THE ROSARY & THE RIFLE

Ernie MacAulay

ACORNPRESS

Charlottetown

2021

AC🞱RNPRESS

Acorn Press
PO Box 22024
Charlottetown, PE
C1A 9J2
Acornpresscanada.com
Printed in Canada
Designed by Cassandra Aragonez
Edited by Ann Thurlow
Copy edit by Jennifer Graham

Library and Archives Canada Cataloguing in PublicationTitle:
The rosary & the rifle / by Ernie MacAulay.
Other titles: Rosary and the rifle
Identifiers: Canadiana (print) 20210173548 | Canadiana (ebook) 20210173580 | ISBN 9781773660721 (softcover) | ISBN 9781773660738 (HTML)

Subjects: LCSH: MacKinnon, Mary Ann. | LCSH: MacKinnon, Mary Ann—Family. | LCSH: MacKinnon, Mary Ann—Death and burial. | LCSH: Murder—Prince Edward Island—Case studies. | LCSH: Murder victims—Prince Edward Island—Biography. | LCSH: Trials (Murder)—Prince Edward Island—Case studies. | LCSH: Murder victims' families—Prince Edward Island—Case studies. | LCSH: Women—Prince Edward Island—Biography. | LCGFT: Biographies.

LCC HV6535.C32 P863 2021 | DDC 364.152/309717—dc23

The publisher acknowledges the support of the Government of Canada, The Canada Council for the Arts and the Province of Prince Edward Island.

CONTENTS

INTRODUCTION 1

MARY ANN'S EARLY LIFE 6

MARRIED LIFE 17

GOING FOR A DRIVE 23

ROSARY INTERRUPTED 42

RIFLE DETAILS REVEALED 57

VERDICT RENDERED 66

POST-TRIAL EVENTS 85

LIFE IN EXILE 95

MACKINNON FAMILY AFTER MARY ANN 100

SOME THOUGHTS 107

ACKNOWLEDGEMENTS 112

INTRODUCTION

THE TOWN OF SOURIS, which was incorporated on November 14, 1910, surrounds a sheltered, and generally ice-free, harbour on Colville Bay. It's on the south side of PEI approximately fifteen miles from the eastern tip of the province. It was first inhabited by the Mi'kmaq people who encamped at what is now the mouth of the Souris River. In 1727, Acadians arrived and established the community as a fishing settlement. The name is the French word for 'mouse'. It is believed to be derived from plagues of mice which came ashore from moored vessels in the early 1700s and attacked the early settlers' crops.

The 1901 census recorded 1,140 residents in the community. The population remained stable over the years. In addition to being a fishing port, Souris was also the main source of supplies for the surrounding agricultural region. In 1951, the town had a post office, a building that housed the town hall, fire hall, and library, a railway station, a branch of the Bank of Commerce, a liquor store, an unlicensed hotel, a branch of the Royal Canadian Legion (with a liquor licence), a movie theatre, two main general stores (the J.J. Hughes Company. Which was on the site of the current Souris Co-op Store, and Matthew and MacLean Limited operated from the current site of the Matthew and MacLean building that has been repurposed), two motor vehicle service stations that were also sub-dealers for Charlottetown automobile franchises, a menswear store, an appliance store, two restaurants, a barber shop, a law office, an Anglican and a Catholic church with associated cemeteries, a public school and a convent, an exhibition grounds, a baseball diamond, and an RCMP Detachment.

The two general stores were open daily six days per week. They were closed on Wednesday afternoons but open until 10:00 PM on Saturdays. Saturday nights were the highlight of the week for the town. After completing their farm chores, residents of the surrounding area came to Souris for their weekly shopping for groceries and other essentials such as kerosene and molasses. Both Hughes' and MacLean's brought in kerosene and molasses in bulk and customers brought their own containers to be filled from barrels. Before the Souris Co-op was established as a 'self-serve' store in the mid-1950s, customers asked for the items that they wished to purchase or provided a shopping list and a store clerk retrieved the items from the store's shelves.

Saturday night was also a social event that was eagerly anticipated each week. With the absence of telephones and very little 'unnecessary' travel, rural residents used a trip to Souris on Saturday nights for both social and practical reasons. Typically, the wives did the grocery shopping and socialized in the stores. Meanwhile the husbands congregated outside to share their stories and discuss current events. These assemblies were held in front of the stores facing Main Street, or, if there was some rum to be shared, behind MacLean's store where there was a coal shed and a horse tie-up area. Typically, the conversations would cover recent weather, current agricultural activities, arrivals and departures of visitors to the area, local and perhaps regional news of interest, local wakes, deaths, and funerals.

But on only an exceptionally rare occasion would the subject matter of these discussions be the motivation for a murder.

There would sometimes be a few farmers using the trip to Souris to drop into Melvin McQuaid's law office occasionally for actual legal advice. But mostly they dropped in for the opportunity to talk to others waiting to see Mel or to get some general advice from him on matters not of a purely legal nature. Mel was a general practitioner and a very generous person. He refrained from sending an invoice for his advice to people who he knew could not afford to pay. The local barber shop was another ideal place to meet your neighbours and discuss local events as you waited in line for a haircut.

The Souris business district was along both sides of Main Street. While the adults were congregating near the two general stores, the lawyer's office, or the barber shop, the youth, who were lucky enough to get to make the trip with their parents, generally gathered in the restaurants or walked back and forth on the sidewalk across from the general stores. In the late 1940s and the early 1950s, three cousins, Susan MacAulay, Estelle MacKinnon, Lorraine MacAulay, and their friend Dorothy 'Dot' MacDonaldcould sometimes be seen along Main Street in Souris on Saturday nights. Dot's older brother, Joey sometimes drove back and forth on Main Street in his father's car and offered the girls a ride. But his main interest was Estelle. Lorraine and Dot both attended Chepstow School and became long-term friends. Apparently inspired by the story or the red-haired orphan in Lucy Maud Montgomery's classic novel, *Anne of Green Gables*, Lorraine and Dot made a childhood pact to be each other's bridesmaids. Lorraine was married on September

3

23, 1952 and asked Dot to be her bridesmaid as agreed but subsequent events caused Dot to decline the offer.

Continuing eastward along Souris' Main Street, a gravel road passed through the community of Chepstow. Then there was a branch road to the right about two miles from Souris to Little Harbour. In 1951, Little Harbour was a farming community with typical farms, ten chains or 660 feet wide, and a nice beach. In earlier times, William F. 'Bill' Power and some business associates operated a lobster canning factory in Little Harbour. Bill was also a successful breeder of silver foxes during the latter period when that industry thrived on PEI. Bill's son, Shady Power, succeeded him as the owner of the Power farmstead. In Little Harbour there was also a pond that, each spring, yielded a harvest of caplin - a small smelt-like fish that could be used as food, bait in lobster traps, or feed for ranched foxes. Only one household had electricity and a telephone. There were a few cottages in the area. But mostly the community was comprised of year-round residents and they were all acquainted with each other. Many were related to each other, either by blood or marriage. Like Souris and the other surrounding areas, Little Harbour residents were largely concerned with matters of local interest and their social contacts were mainly local.

Travelling westbound from Little Harbour to Souris provides the traveller with a view of Chepstow Point on the left. This 'postcard perfect' scene includes a piece of farmland that extends southward to the Northumberland Strait, framed by one of PEI's famously beautiful red cliffs. The view is especially majestic on a sunny day when seen from the elevation provided by the farm that George MacAulay bought from Ralph Mooney in the late 1940s about a half mile east of Chepstow Point. George's sister was called Mary Ann.

The farmland on Chepstow Point has been owned by a MacDonald family since PEI was settled by Europeans. At the time of these events, Aeneas P. MacDonald, son of Gabriel MacDonald, and known as 'Aeneas Gab', because he was 'Gab Donald's' son, farmed the land on Chepstow Point. Aeneas and his wife Catherine, also called Katey, were relatively prosperous and progressive farmers. Aeneas was among the first owners of a car and a farm tractor in the region. Like other area farmers at the time, although he had a tractor, Aeneas also had a general-purpose horse for winter travel and small farm tasks that were unsuitable for a tractor. Although at least two of his neighbours were known to have participated in 'rum running' during prohibition years, Aeneas did not participate in such initiatives. Aeneas and Katey were devout Catholics who also supported their community. Aeneas volunteered as one of the three trustees for Chepstow school district and when the district needed a site for a new school, Aeneas donated an acre of land for the purpose. Their son, Joey, lived at home with them and assisted with the farm work.

CHAPTER 1

MARY ANN'S EARLY LIFE

AENEAS MACAULAY married Susan Jane Mooney on November 26, 1901 and farmed land that he inherited from his father, Michael MacAulay, in St. Catherines, approximately two miles east of Souris. Aeneas also fished lobsters during May and June each year off Chepstow. As was typical in the era, Susan did not work outside the home.

Aeneas and Susan had six sons and one daughter. Mary Ann, the second youngest child, was born on November 4, 1909. Mary Ann had older brothers George, Joe, Albert, Frank, and Clarence and a younger brother, Charlie.

Front Row – George, Joe, Albert
Back row – Frank, Clarence, Charlie,
with Mary Ann digitally inserted.

6

Susan MacAulay died on October 1, 1911 when Mary Ann was less than two years old. Mr. and Mrs. John MacDonald cared for her for two years. Then, at the age of four, the sisters of the Congregation of Notre Dame took her into St. Mary's Convent in Souris. Her care was paid for by her uncle, Augustus MacAulay. 'Uncle Gus' was Aeneas MacAulay's brother and a prosperous resident of Springfield, Massachusetts.

The following is taken from a Springfield, Mass. exchange and Mr. MacAulay is known by many Island people having been born near Souris, PEI.

His first wife Sadie Croken was a sister of Dr. T.E. Croken, V.G., of Charlottetown, and Mrs. Jas. B. Croken, Summerfield near this place. Mr. MacAulay paid a visit to the Island last summer, and looked the picture of health, strong and robust. He was highly esteemed in Springfield, Mass., and wherever known. Many Island people who met him at his house was always speaking of him being a credit to the Island and to his friends. The funeral of Augustus MacAulay, 62, of Belvedere Street, who died yesterday in Fitchburg, will be held at the home Monday morning at 8:15 followed by Solemn Requiem high Mass at the Holy Name church at 9. Burial will be in St. Michael's Cemetery. Mr. MacAulay, for many years a superintendent of construction for the New England Telephone and Telegraph company, was found dead yesterday morning in his room at Hotel Raymond in Fitchburg. It is believed that death was due to heart attack sometime during the night.

Mr. MacAulay had been connected with the company in various capacities for the past 40 years and had attained wide recognition for his accomplishments as construction

superintendent. Especially notable was his work in connection with the reconstruction work in Vermont and New
Hampshire following the disastrous flood on November
1929. Hundreds of miles of lines were put out of commission by the flood were restrung and resumption of service
throughout the flood-stricken area was made possible
largely through his efforts.

Born near Souris, Prince Edward Island, Mr. MacAulay
started work for the Telephone company in 1888. He began as a lineman and rose to be district foreman, district
plant chief and supervisor of outside construction. He was
past president of the William J Denver chapter, Telephone
Pioneers of America, and served recently as president of
the Public Service association of Springfield. He was a
member of the Tuesday Club, of the Knights of Columbus
and of Springfield Lodge of Elks. He was a very active
member of the Holy Name Society of Holy Name Church.

Mr. MacAulay leaves his widow, Mrs. Mary A (Campbell)
MacAulay of this city, one sister Mrs. Joseph (Josephine)
Steele of Canada, and several nephews and nieces.

Mr. MacAulay's first wife Sadie (Croken) MacAulay, died
fifteen years ago. He married his second wife, Mary A
(Campbell) MacAulay seven years ago."

Although a good student and well cared for by the nuns
at St. Mary's Convent, life was lonely for a young girl sep-
arated from her father and siblings. On February 27, 1915,
Mary Ann wrote the following

"Dear Papa,

This is my first letter to write to you.

I am able to read and spell and sew. We learn so many things here. We are able to be very good here.

I learn Catechism and will make my First Communion in the spring. The Mothers are all kind to me and I'm very happy with all the girls.

Sending kisses and love to you.
Please write me.
I am your little girl.

Mary MacAulay"

St. Mary's Convent, opened in 1881; Annex built in 1919.

St. Mary's Convent class of 1916/17
with Mary Ann MacAulay on the right end of the first row.

Mary Ann lived and studied at the convent until she completed grade ten in 1924. Mary Ann then attended Notre Dame Convent in Charlottetown for two years and obtained her first-class teacher's certificate. She taught in one-room schools in Souris West and Little Harbour, PEI for two years each and married John Charles 'JC' MacKinnon on July 1, 1931.

Education in the Convent provided Mary Ann with an exposure to music and a better understanding of literature and poetry than was provided in the secular schools of the era. The nuns encouraged their students to develop any musical aptitude they had; Mary Ann learned to play the organ and she enjoyed literature and poetry. This somewhat classical education shaped her philosophical outlook on life, gave her a love of music, and a life-long interest in writing.

This interest followed her after she left the   Convent. In her adult years, Mary Ann discussed her life and her philosophy of life in a story submitted to a 'True Story Contest' in New York:

"An Outlaw Among In-laws"

Strange after all these years and after many feeble attempts of blurting it all out on paper, here I am at 2:30 in the morning to begin this story which is my life. I have been knitting, reading, mending children's stockings up until now, me of my splurges which I take occasionally and now I'm winding it up starting this story. It will take me many nights but I am bound I will get it in print bit by bit. I hope somebody else reads and from it draws some bit of solace at least solace, to know that somebody else lived and conquered. Maybe right now you feel as if you will never see a bright spot, dark clouds are all around and insurmountable at that, well believe me it will get bright. I too have walked that path and the path of utter hopelessness. If you can see even one little glimmer of the star of love guide yourself by it and in the end it will conquer. My guiding star was pretty feeble by times and I had my moments I felt like throwing it all up and refusing to carry on another moment. You will break and break again but do not give up. The one who said, "There is a silver lining in every cloud" sure knew what they were talking about. Now to get along with my story and cut to the details.

When I got married, I was a young school teacher, carefree, happy and with only the ordinary every day ups and downs of life to bother me. I was brought up for the most part in a Convent, as a matter of fact eleven years of my life were spent there. My mother died when I was scarcely two years old. I was the only girl and only sister for six more brothers. They were all older, except one brother Charlie who was just four months old when our mother died. We weren't well off so our father had to close our home and go away to Halifax to make a living. We were all scattered out. A cousin of ours, Mrs. John MacDonald, took me and my brother Clarence was taken next door or next farm. I should say by a sister (Mrs. John MacInnis) of this cousin that took me. So we spent a part of our lives together. The year

or two before I went to the Convent and then all my
vacations until father married again which was ten
years after mother's death. It was an uncle, Augustus
MacAulay, my father's brother, who paid for my education in the Convent. He was married in Springfield,
Mass and was quite well off. He had no family of his
own. He was an official at the telephone company.
It was while visiting one summer that he suggested
placing me in the Convent. So you see I was brought
up in a sort of sheltered and loving atmosphere. I
was an only girl so my father (Aeneas MacAulay) and
brothers, all six of them (George, Joe, Albert, Frank,
Clarence and Charlie) got to look upon their Mary
Ann as something very special. I was the apple of
Uncle Gus's eye too and also of my foster parents
Mr. and Mrs. John Andrew MacDonald as they too
had no children of their own. I seemed always to be
able to make my way, even in the Convent the sisters
were more than good to me and to this day that kind
of love is there and these same sisters who taught
me have proved my tower of strength and consolation when in trouble. Of course I do not mean in the
teachers I had but two in particular have held me as
their very own all through the years and I have sobbed
out my story more than once to these. To me, M. St.
M. Justin, it had to be in a letter as she was moved
and made minister of novices in her mother house in
Montreal but the other, M. Saint Vincent of the Rosary
has been here at our St. Mary's Convent in Souris for
years. She is like a faithful old beacon to me. I can go
to her at any time for comfort and consolation.

"I had a step-mother, in fact. Father is dead and
has been dead since May 1929."

Unfortunately, the contest submission ended abruptly in
mid-sentence before Mary Ann had the opportunity to tell
us about her life with her in-laws during the first couple of
years of her marriage to JC. The undated cover sheet that
was to accompany the submission to New York was titled
"Life with in-laws" but Mary Ann did not reach that phase
of her life in the chronological account of her life that she
had written. Perhaps some traumatic event intervened
and prevented her from reaching what was to be the es-
sence of her submission. Although we never actually find
out, there is a suggestion that there might have been some
conflicts in the relationship she had with her in-laws. The
details we have show a spunky lady who resorted to optimism to overcome the disappointments of life.

Mary Ann's education by sisters of the Congregation of
Notre Dame exposed her to the works of some great poets
which she made reference to in her own writing. She had
an appreciation of good literature, especially poetry, and
turned her own hand to writing verse. This one she called
"Memories of 1927 – 1928. To J.C. McKinnon From M.A.M.":

My Blarney Boy

I

You can talk of your beauty
Of your sons devoted to duty,
But give to me my blarney boy
And I have a world of joy.

II

Sept 23rd 27 was our meeting day,
And very little paved the way,
One short drive sent the dart
The letter pierced it in my heart.
Human nature has its joys and pains
But few where true love reigns,
We have our little spats too,
But they soon absorb like the dew
When the sun of love beams full and strong,
No quarrel can last for long.

III

So talk away of your beauty,
Of your devoted ones to duty,
But I take my blarney boy,
Of my life, the pride and joy.

She followed the first poem with this:

A *Beautiful Name*:

"J" is for judgment a plenteous store,
"C" is for cuteness couldn't have more,
"M" is for mildness in every plight,
"C" is for courage to do what is right,
"K" is for kindness to young and old,
"I" is for ideals brilliant as gold,
"N" is for nonsense lots of it there,
"N" is for naughtiness and some to spare,
"O" is for opinions always true and sane,
"N" is for niceness and not in vain.
Together they make a world to me dear
And will mean more at some future year.

Mary Ann married her "Blarney Boy" with the "Beautiful Name". They lived with JC's parents on a farm near where she was born in St. Catherines for a couple of years before moving to a farm in nearby Little Harbour.

CHAPTER 2
MARRIED LIFE

MARY ANN MARRIED 'JC' MacKinnon on July 1, 1931   at St. Mary's Church in Souris. They lived on JC's farm in Little Harbour, PEI and had twelve children. The first, Mary Estelle (who was always known by her middle name) was born in 1932. The youngest, David, was born in 1947 – twelve children in just fifteen years.

Front Row Left to Right: Margie Oberthier, Maureen Howlett, Betty Fay, Alice Bushey, and Estelle MacAulay. Back Row: Obie, Danny, Aelred, David, Kenny, and Justin MacKinnon.

Though she was a busy farmer's wife, Mary Ann submitted a weekly column to The Charlottetown Patriot entitled "Mrs. Wiggs and Her Garden Patch" (A sprig of this, a sprig of that from Souris and vicinity). The actual author was not identified in the submissions with readers left to guess the identity of "Mrs. Wiggs". Typically, the issues covered included social activities, visits of people from other places, visits by local people to other places, weddings, births, deaths, and other similar events in eastern Kings County. But sometimes she reported on a wide variety of other subjects such as the price of local goods. There were also some occasions when Mary Ann expressed her personal philosophies. And she also used the forum to express her displeasure with the state of the education system.

In 1947, 'Mrs. Wiggs' noted that entries in an old diary from the late 19th century showed pork was about ten cents a pound, firewood cost about $2.00 per cord, and skilled labour was about 75 to 85 cents a day. Mrs. Wiggs also noted that an 1888 entry in the diary showed that the writer's annual "school bill" was 45 cents plus a load of wood, cut and split, valued at 50 cents, for a total of 95 cents.

She then stated: "When you then look at this last item dated 1888 for a school bill of .95 cts you wonder if it doesn't compare a little bit with present day. Everything including the teachers (especially in our country schools) is tried to be kept down to a .95 ct basis. This 95 cts might have bought something back there in 1888 but not too much does it buy this 1947. While on the subject of teachers we must say also

'More power to the teachers in Charlottetown at long last they received a raise in salary.' It seems funny this question of teachers and money never seems to mix. People just think they should be a self-sacrificing group out for giving their all for little or no recompense. All very well but to be educated for a teacher costs money and there are very few who do not like to have enough to eat and sufficient clothing to wear. At the salary some country teachers get it is just nip and tuck to do that."

In July 1947 Mrs. Wiggs observed that some warm weather had given the promise that "We will have something in the cellar and granary this fall after all." Noting a "fairly plentiful" crop of wild strawberries that summer and some Islanders' propensity to celebrate with alcohol, she paraphrased a bit of Burns' poetry by saying: 'Gie fools their silks and knaves their wine, Prince Edward Island is Prince Edward Island for a' that.'" Apparently not in complete agreement with the famous poet's advice, she provided some advice to Islanders:

"We have a wonderful little Island here but idle dreams and empty boasting will not get us anywhere. We must not sit by and watch for nature to do it all like ripening the strawberries on the hill and so on. We must work hard in hand with nature and develop our country and our talents to the fullest so as more of our sons and daughters will have a good living right here and will not have to seek their fortune in other lands."

In a January 1948 column, Mrs. Wiggs provided details of a Christmas concert held in Little Harbour School on December 19, 1947 under the guidance of teacher Lorraine

MacAulay. She wrote: "*The students acquitted themselves very well considering the fact it is some years since they had a concert and it proved a very nice and enjoyable program.*" After noting the contributions of both students and outside entertainers she commented that Santa arrived but "[h]is whiskers did look awfully in need of some Halo shampoo and his clothes did look the worse for wear but he was his same jolly old self."

In the same column we learn about the amount of snow that had fallen to that point in the 1947/48 winter and are advised that

"*It would be a fine time to take up John G. Whittier's poem Snowbound and re-read it. You will enjoy it and before you have many lines read you will find yourself living again those days with your rugged ancestors. Somehow after reading it that bit of snow covering your front steps or front sidewalk will seem very trifling.*"

After concluding that there could be more to discuss than snow, Mrs. Wiggs metaphorically discussed a crude method of confining potentially wandering cattle to their assigned spaces, which led to a philosophical discussion of confining common people to their assigned spaces through pricing.

"*In days gone by the farmer who had a cow bad to jump fences had a method of dealing with her. He tied a piece of board from her horns and which covered her eyes. The poor cow was a bit in distress but what could she do about it only submit to her master's authority? It served its purpose, this* board, and kept the cow from getting into greener pastures. We are much the same nowadays. Somebody was afraid we common folk were getting too close to greener fields so up goes the prices on everything. When we ask questions we are blinded by a lot of facts and figures which to us are meaningless. So like the cow with this board on our eyes, we go placidly on picking the bits of grass here and there that our higher masters leave us. This old time method of the cow and the board is pretty well out-dated. Some have chose electric fences to keep their cows and animals in check. Maybe it is time some of us reversed the whole process and took the electric current in our own hands and turned the heat on those responsible for those higher prices. If it keeps on the cosmetic counters will have something more to sell than attar of roses or eau de Cologne. It will read something like this on the labels: eau de bacon and attar of butter. If we do not get the taste we will at least have the aroma."

Mrs. Wiggs' writings not only identify her as an astute observer and chronicler of local events, educational issues, agricultural practices, and economic issues but also that Mary Ann was one of Mother Nature's admirers and a person inclined to optimism where it could be found. In one of her columns she wrote:

"Two prisoners looked from behind bars, one saw mud, the other stars. That is pretty much the situation on some of our by-roads here on P.E.I. But do not look out and 'addmire' the road but admire the beautiful colorings of our trees. They are a marvelous sight just now.

The very beauty of them to thrill a person through and leave a warm and satisfying glow. Old mother nature, or rather should we not say the Creator of all these things, knew His business and gave us all these to delight and inspire us to higher and greater things.

Even following J.C.'s death, Mary Ann continued to be optimistic about her future and the future of her community. One of her frequent sayings was: "Little Harbour will bloom again."

But could this optimism carry Mary Ann through the next phase of her life?

CHAPTER 3
GOING FOR A DRIVE

ON JULY 10, 1951 Joseph Gabriel 'Joey' MacDonald and a neighbour, Arnold Bernard MacDonald, spent the day driving around eastern Kings County, PEI in a car owned by Joey's father, Aeneas MacDonald of Chepstow. MacDonald is a very common name on PEI so often people were given nicknames to tell them apart. These nicknames were based on the names of fathers or even grandfathers. Joey's father was named Aeneas and his paternal grandfather was named Gabriel but went by the nickname 'Gab'. Aeneas was commonly referred to as "Aeneas Gab". Joey was known as "Joey Gab" and also as "Joey Aeneas". But he was most commonly called Joey Gab. Arnold MacDonald was known as "Arnold Walter Allan". Both were farm boys who lived with their families with one farm separating them. Although they shared a surname, they were not blood relatives.

Mary Ann's oldest child, Estelle, was 19 years old in 1951. A very attractive young lady, Estelle had graduated from Grade 11 (which was high school matriculation at the time) at St. Mary's Convent. She spent the 1950-51 academic year teaching in a one-room school in Kingsboro, a few miles east of the MacKinnon home in Little Harbour. During the school year, Estelle boarded with a widow, Ethel MacLean, in Kingsboro.

On July 10, 1951 Estelle travelled by bus from her home to visit with her former landlady. At about 7:15 PM, Ethel

MacLean left her house and travelled to Souris to watch a movie and left Estelle alone in the house.

The events which followed Mrs. MacLean's departure are documented in the transcript of a preliminary hearing for a charge of attempted rape which was subsequently laid against Joey MacDonald. Preliminary hearings are conducted to determine if there is sufficient evidence to commit an accused person to stand trial for an indictable offence. The test for committal to trial is relatively easy for the Crown to achieve: there must be some evidence upon which a reasonable jury properly instructed could return a verdict of guilty. Unlike today where the Crown has a constitutional duty to disclose all of its evidence to the accused, there was no requirement for Crown disclosure at the time of these events and defence counsel relied on preliminary hearings to become informed of the evidence they would have to rebut at the trial. As well, it was an opportunity for both sides to test their witnesses in a courtroom setting. The preliminary hearing was held on August 1, 1951 before J.W. MacDonald, KC, Stipendiary Magistrate for Kings County, in Georgetown. Magistrates were the equivalent of today's provincial court judges and stipendiary magistrates were not full-time workers but were paid by the cases heard and processes (such as summonses and subpoenae) issued.

Herbert Hedley Fraser offered testimony. He was a farmer who lived across the road from Mrs. MacLean. He said that he was on the ronad between his farm and the MacLean place, attending to mechanical problems with a cousin's car. He saw a car drive into the farmyard at approximately 8:00 PM. Mr. Fraser identified the occupants of the vehicle as Joey Gab and Arnold Walter but he could not say who drove the car into the yard. He saw the men enter the house and, approximately ten minutes later, he heard a girl's screams coming from the MacLean house. He could not identify the girl who screamed. But moments later Joey Gab "... had her by the arm, his other arm around her and he was whacking her into the car". When asked about the girl's actions, he said "She was leaning back considerable." Deputy Attorney General J.O.C. Campbell, KC along with S.S. Hessian, represented the Crown in the proceeding. With a series of leading questions, he established that Mr. Fraser knew that Estelle MacKinnon had taught in Kingsboro School the previous academic year and boarded with Mrs. MacLean. In cross examination, defence counsel H.F. MacPhee, KC assisted by Souris lawyer Melvin J. McQuaid, established that Mr. Fraser recognized the car as one that Joey Gab drove and had driven to the MacLean property on a number of occasions in the past. He also established that people in the community knew that Joey was going with Estelle. Defence counsel ended his cross examination by suggesting that what Mr. Fraser witnessed was ordinary youthful male/female interaction where the female "... hangs back coyly". Mr. Fraser stated that he was married and the type of behaviour he saw was not something that he had personally experienced.

In the same proceeding, Ethel MacLean testified that Estelle MacKinnon had boarded with her while she taught at the Kingsboro School the previous academic year. In response to Mr. Campbell's question about Estelle's character, Mrs. MacLean responded "I considered her a sweet good girl". Mrs. Mac-Lean then testified that, when she returned from seeing a movie in Souris at almost 11:00 PM, Estelle was not at her house. She arrived about fifteen or twenty minutes later. When Estelle came in, Mrs. MacLean lit a lamp (as she had no electricity, it would have been a kerosene lamp) and started a fire in the kitchen stove. Mrs. MacLean testified that Joey Gab's car was in the yard and that Estelle "... was very pale. I knew that she had been crying." Mrs. Mac-Lean said Estelle was wearing a yellow blouse and a black skirt and "She looked mussed; her clothing was mussed."

During cross examination by Mr. MacPhee, Mrs. MacLean testified that Joey Gab usually picked up Estelle at her house on Friday evenings and returned her there on Sunday evenings. On a few occasions, he visited on weekdays. Mrs. MacLean said she was always in bed when Estelle returned on Sunday evenings.

In response to Mr. MacPhee's question about how she knew that Estelle had been crying, Mrs. MacLean testified: "Her eyes were red, and all signs of tears on her face, traces of tears. There is a look when a person is crying." When questioned about a possible lover's quarrel, Mrs. MacLean testified, that she knew that Estelle did not want to continue going out with Joey.

Arnold Bernard MacDonald, commonly known as Arnold Walter Allan, was age 18 at the time of the hearin. He testified that he had been driving around with Joey Gab all day on July 10, 1951; that they drove east as far as North Lake. They drank a couple of quarts of moonshine, called at a number of places throughout the day, and experienced some mechanical problems which they had repaired at a local mechanic's premises. Arnold testified that they were near the MacLean residence and just decided to call there for a visit. He said that Joey was driving his father's car. They drove near the entrance platform and Estelle met them at the door. She came out of the house and sat on the steps. He said that they had talked for a short period, and while still talking, "The two of them were standing up; he had his arms around her. Don't know if he was hugging. They came to the car. He told me to drive."

Arnold then testified, "They got in the car. He still had his arms around her." Arnold said Joey and Estelle were talking but he claimed that he could not hear what they were saying although all three were sitting in the front seat. Arnold said there was no significance to the fact he was driving. He claimed that he had driven the vehicle the day before and "We took spells" driving.

Arnold then testified that he drove the car to Aeneas MacDonald's farm then drove approximately ⅛ of a mile along a private road, through a swampy area, and stopped the vehicle. During cross-examination, Arnold testified that Joey and Estelle had been keeping company for almost a year. He provided a different reason for driving the car between the MacLean residence and the MacDonald farm claiming that it was his proximity to the steering wheel that was the reason he drove the vehicle away from the MacLean residence. Arnold testified that, when he stopped the vehicle, he got out and Estelle said "Thanks Arnold" and he left the area with Joey and Estelle sitting in the front seat of the car and walked home.

The Crown then called two doctors to testify. Dr. Joseph A. McMillan, who practiced family medicine in

Charlottetown, PEI, examined Estelle MacKinnon on July 12, 1951. Dr. McMillan had Dr. John Maloney, a practicing gynecologist: assist him in conducting the examination. Dr. McMillan testified that he found "... bruises in the following locations: Left side of the forehead, left arm, small one on the right forearm, bruises on both thighs, large one 3 inches on the left thigh, obviously recent. An X-ray of the chest area did not show any evidence of a fractured rib. In cross-examination by Mr. MacPhee, Dr. McMillan explained that he identified the bruises as being recent because absorption of blood had not yet taken place. Dr. McMillan also explained that all bruises are circular in nature "...unless made by some specific type of instrument". He also provided more specific locations of the bruises.

Dr. Maloney testified that he had been practicing medicine for nine years with a specialization in gynecology. He stated that he also examined Estelle MacKinnon on July 12, 1951 and found: "Swelling on the forehead over both eyes, large bruise on the left arm; large bruise on the right forearm; bruises on both thighs; small bruise on right leg. And then I did a pelvic examination: The hymen membrane at the entrance of the vagina or passage had recently been torn and bled on touching." Dr. Maloney was unable to provide any opinion on the methodology associated with the torn hymen. Dr. Maloney stated that there was no external bleeding but bleeding started on opening the passage. During cross-examination, Dr. Maloney explained the basis for his conclusion was that the injury was recent. "The reason we say a thing is torn recently is, if it has been torn a while little clots form in the blood vessels and they no longer bleed. But in the first three days it will bleed again." When asked if the membrane was slightly torn or completely ruptured, Dr. Maloney responded "Roughly, a tear about ¼ inch long."

Dr. McMillan was present during Dr. Maloney's testimony and the Crown recalled him and Dr. McMillan expressed agreement with Dr. Maloney's findings.

Deputy Attorney General Campbell called Estelle MacKinnon to testify on behalf of the Crown. Estelle testified that she was at Mrs. MacLean's residence on July 10, 1951. She heard someone coming up the steps but did not recall hearing a knock on the door. Joey MacDonald came into the kitchen and asked to wash his hands. Arnold MacDonald had remained in the car and, while Joey was washing his hands, Estelle went out to the front steps and talked to him. When Joey finished washing his hands, he came outside and sat on the steps beside Estelle and asked her to go for a drive with him. Estelle replied "We were all through two weeks previously". She stated Joey then said, "You are coming" and then, "He grabbed me by the left arm first and then he had his both arms around me." She then described being dragged to the car. Joey then tried to pull her into the car. The car door slammed against her left arm, causing her to scream. She said that she was crying at the time and when "He saw that he could not drag me into the car, he jumped out and batted me over the head 5 or 6 times."

Estelle testified that Joey told Arnold to drive and asked him to speed the vehicle up two or three times along the route. Arnold drove the car onto Aeneas MacDonald's farm. When they entered a swampy area, he said he doubted he would be able to drive through it. Joey told him to "Get through it; get through it somehow."

It was almost dusk when Joey asked Arnold to stop the car and told him he could go "... that is all I want of you". Estelle did not say that she thanked Arnold before he left as he had earlier testified. Estelle said that, after Arnold left, Joey spoke a few decent words to her. Then forced he into the back seat of the car saying, "I just had to see you tonight ...I was going to get you somewhere." She said Joey had been drinking and that she was terrified and crying and he said, "I would get you somewhere, supposing it was Mt. Stewart, Georgetown, or anywhere" and, "I was going to get something off you here tonight for all the trouble you have put me through". Estelle testified that Joey then said he was going to rape her.

He "flattened me down in the back seat ... unbuttoned his pants and tore them half off ... Then he pulled my skirt up and tried to spread my legs out and hold me down with his other hand. When I was screeching he had his hand over my mouth. Then he tore my pants right in two, and his penis entered my body three or four times. After all that struggling I opened the car door and got out."

Estelle testified that she repeatedly said, "You are killing me" and, Joey replied, "No, it won't hurt". She also said that, after she got out of the car and tried to walk, she fell twice.

Estelle then testified that there were two quart-sized moonshine bottles in the vehicle, one empty and the other partly filled. Joey threw both bottles into a nearby hedge. One of the bottles broke. He did this in an exchange for a promise to Estelle that she would "get home alive" (as the Crown Attorney phrased it) and go with Joey until she moved to Charlottetown in September to begin training to become a nurse. She also testified that she went to the scene later with the RCMP and they located a broken bottle and an empty bottle.

Crown Counsel then asked Estelle if Joey had ever done anything to make her afraid of him. Estelle said that they had previous quarrels and had previously broken up. She also said, on an earlier occasion, Joey had arrived in her room at the MacLean household and she feared for her life because he showed her a revolver that he had in his pocket and told her the history of the weapon. Because she feared for her life, she chose to officially break up with him on June 27, 1951 by telling him in front of her mother who tried to reason with Joey. He left the MacKinnon residence about 11:30 PM. He returned about an hour later and Estelle and Mary Ann reported the matter to the Souris Detachment of the RCMP.

The enquiry returned to the night in question. Estelle testified she and Joey left the field in the car. They drove to Walter MacDonald's (Arnold's father) farm where Joey went in for a drink of water. Then he drove her to Mrs. MacLean's to get some belongings. Then he drove her back to her own house and she went in. Mary Ann was home and made something to eat but Estelle did not eat anything. Estelle described her clothing as a torn slip and blouse, grease-stained and dirty. Her skirt was all wrinkled. The Crown then presented the blouse, skirt, and slip that Estelle wore on July 10 as evidence. Estelle testified she had burned her torn underpants when she returned home that night.

Mr. MacPhee cross-examined Estelle and she agreed that she had been keeping company with Joey but "not steady" until she broke it off on June 27, 1951. Estelle also confirmed that her mother was there when she told Joey their relationship was over. She agreed with counsel's suggestion that her mother was "... not feeling very kindly disposed to Joe" and had asked the RCMP to arrest him later that night.

Mr. MacPhee then asked Estelle to talk more about her relationship with Joey. She said she had begun keeping fairly regular company with him in August 1950. Estelle had seen Joey at a dance, and had danced with him on an occasion between June 27 and July 10, 1950. Mr. MacPhee then reviewed the details of Estelle's entry into the car at Mrs. MacLean's house. He reminded her of Mr. Fraser's evidence that Joey had her by one arm and had his other arm around her. In the manner of a skilled defence counsel, Mr. MacPhee had Estelle agree that she "got in" the car, significantly minimizing the previous evidence of a significant struggle and a forceful entry to the vehicle MacPhee then established that, although they had never parked in the particular place that was chosen on July 10, Estelle and Joey had previously parked in other locations. He suggested these spots "... would be utilized with love making" but Estelle rejected the suggestion of love making and answered "None whatsoever". Estelle agreed with counsel's description of his client as being "extremely passionate" but she "... always tried to reason with him and talk things out on a human basis with him". During further questioning, Estelle stated that, on some occasions, Joey had pulled up her dress and she told him to go away and never come

back. Defence counsel then established "other familiarities" such as Joey putting his hand on Estelle's thigh be-
neath her dress.

Mr. MacPhee then questioned her on the issue of
Arnold's departure from the scene of the alleged attempted rape. Estelle testified that she did not recall saying
"Thank you Arnold" but said she could not "... outwardly
deny [saying] it".

In Canadian criminal proceedings, all accused persons are entitled 'to make full answer and defence' of the
charge(s) they are facing. Defence counsel are required to
treat the court and witnesses with courtesy and respect
and represent clients resolutely, honourably, and within
the limits of the law. Defence counsel sometimes have to
embark on difficult lines of questioning of witnesses in
order to discharge their responsibilities to their clients.
The following excerpt from the transcript of the preliminary hearing reveals the difficult line of questioning Mr.
MacPhee engaged in in his cross examination of Estelle:

19.   **Mary Estelle MacKinnon**   **3.**
Cross-ex

Q. Arnold left and you and Joe started a conversation. You say the conversation in the beginning was much like his conversation used to be, - like old times. That is what you meant to express?
A. Yes, it expressed he was going to have me whether I wanted or not.

Q. He would suggest to you he was very fond of you?
A. Yes

Q. And I believe you had been very fond of him? You would not have been going with him otherwise?
A. I was for a time, yes.

20.   **Mary Estelle MacKinnon**   **4.**
Cross-ex

Q. Would there be any exchange of presents between you?
A. Yes.

Q. Did Joe ever give you gifts?
A. Yes, Christmas mainly.

Q. What was the nature of your birthday gift?
A. A camera.

Q. Had you given any gifts to Joe?
A. At Christmas.

Q. So that you were on the level of two people who were keeping Company, exchanging gifts?
A. Right.

Q. Then coming back to that event of Arnold leaving you; he says you thanked him, and you say you and Joe sat for a while talking in the front seat. You said, "there was some decent conversation". And when asked about that, you said it was like old times?
A. It was very few words.

Q. Afterwards both of you got into the back seat. You say he Helped you?
A. He pushed me in the back seat.

Q. That is where this alleged rape took place?
A. Yes.

Q. You were lying down in the back seat?
A. He flattened me out in the back seat.

Q. You were lying on your back in the back seat?
A. Yes.

Q. And you spoke of Joe's habit of kissing you. Did he do that on this occasion?
A. Yes; putting his hand on my mouth so I would not cry out. It was the same incident.

Q. And he made love to you generally?
A. No.

Q. Didn't he tell you he wanted you badly?
A. He said he wanted me.

Q. He kissed you, and you told me before these kisses were generally mutual between you kissed back?
A. Not this time.

Q. He attempted other familiarities with you. You spoke of his habit of getting his hand under your dress and putting it on your thigh. Did he put his hand under your dress on this occasion?
A. He grabbed my skirt and pulled it up.

Q. And you say he had one hand on your mouth?
A. Not all the time. I was screaming trying to get clear of him.

Q. This was in the back seat of the car?
A. Yes.

Q. As you say, he took his pants off?
A. Yes, and before the act was completed I think they were all off.

Q. Have you ever had an experience like that before?
A. No.

Q. You never had any intercourse with a man?
A. Never

Q. Such an experience was entirely foreign to you?
A. It certainly was.

Q. When you say he put his penis into your private parts 3 or 4 times why do you make that statement? Was it from what you felt?
A. Yes

Q. And you had never any such experience before?
A. Never.

Q. So that you felt some little soreness?
A. It was killing me. He grabbed hold of me with his hand on my private parts. I thought he was trying to tear me apart.

Q. Is it because you felt this soreness that you knew he had connection with you?
A. No, I felt the connection I knew his penis entered my body.

21. Mary Estelle MacKinnon 5.
Cross-ex

Q. Doctors tell me that a girl without previous experience would not know. You say you actually felt his penis enter your body. Are you swearing that?
A. Yes.

Q. You heard the doctor say the Hymen was perforated a quarter of an inch. Do you mean to say the penis entered your body now in face of medical evidence and went in 3 or 4 times?
A. He tried to get it in 3 or 4 times. I could feel it. I felt it was killing me.

Although Joey's lawyer asked these questions in a fair and honourable way and consistent with his duty to advance his client's interests to the fullest extent that the law permitted, they must have been exceptionally traumatic for a young and angelic witness such as Estelle.

Mr. MacPhee then questioned Estelle about what happened next. He established that they visited to Walter MacDonald's for a drink of water and that they visited Mrs. MacLean's to pick up Estelle's sweater, billfold, and some strawberries and the subsequent activities at the MacKinnon household. Under further questioning, Estelle admitted that she had made a date with Joey to call for her the following afternoon and take her to the Souris Regatta.

She said Joey arrived at about 11:30 the following morning but she asked him, "How can I go anywhere feeling the way I am?" Estelle explained she agreed to go out again with Joey only because she was terrified of him – so terrified that she "... would do anything to get clear of him. Stalling for time." She said she neither went to the regatta with Joey nor had any intention of doing so when she agreed to the date.

Estelle then recounted the events of the rest of the day. She and her mother went to seek advice from her pastor, Monsignor James A. Murphy, PH of St. Mary's Parish in Souris. He was not at home so they went to the regatta to find him. Apparently, they did not find their pastor until that evening, then they, following the pastor's advice, reported the matter to the RCMP and then sought medical attention at the request of the police.

The Crown then called Cpl. Lionel F.M. Strong who was in charge of Souris Detachment of the RCMP. Cpl. Strong testified that, at about 8:30 PM on July 11, 1951 he, Estelle MacKinnon, Mary Ann MacKinnon, and Cst. Ralph Sandberg drove 350 to 400 yards along a road beside Aeneas MacDonald's farm. There he located a black straw hat and a black felt hat which the Crown entered as evidence. Cpl. Strong testified that he was directed to look by two trees along the line fence of the farm where he found parts of a broken bottle at the bottom of a tree and small pieces of glass sticking out of the tree.

He also found a bottle about five feet from the base of the tree. Cpl. Strong then testified that, on the following day, July 12, he took possession of a slip, skirt, and blouse worn by Estelle MacKinnon on July 10. He also said that, on July 13, Estelle MacKinnon laid a charge of rape against Joseph Gabriel MacDonald and a warrant was issued for his arrest.

At approximately 8:30 PM on Sunday, July 15, 1951, Melvin J. McQuaid, brought the accused to the Souris Detachment where Cpl. Strong formally took him into custody under the warrant that the court had issued. Cpl. Strong testified that RCMP members had been looking for MacDonald since the afternoon of July 13 but were unable to locate him. Cpl. Strong also testified that he had the articles of clothing examined at the Public Health Centre in Charlottetown, PEI but no seminal stains were found.

In his cross-examination of Cpl. Strong, Mr. MacPhee confirmed that Mary Ann MacKinnon and Estelle MacKinnon had made the complaint to the police, had turned in the items of clothing, and had accompanied the police to the scene where the bottle and bottle fragments were recovered. Cpl. Strong agreed with Mr. MacPhee's suggestion that there were no tears in the skirt and there was a tear or rip in the slip under one arm. As its last witness, the Crown called Cst. Ralph B. Sandberg, also of the Souris Detachment of the RCMP. Cst. Sandberg stated that he had accompanied Cpl. Strong, had heard his evidence, and agreed with Cpl. Strong's testimony. In addition, Cst. Sandberg testified that he had found a watch in a hay field approximately four or five feet from where Cpl. Strong had found the two hats.

The prosecution concluded its case at 1:30 PM on August 1, 1951 and defence counsel elected not to call any evidence. Stipendiary Magistrate MacDonald administered the customary invitation to testify and warning:

"Having heard the evidence, do you wish to say anything in answer to the charge? You are not bound to say anything, but whatever you say will be taken down in writing and may be given in evidence against you at your trial. You must clearly understand that you have nothing to hope from any promise or favour and nothing to fear from any threat which may have been held out to you to induce you to make any admission or confession of guilt, but whatever you now say may be given in evidence against you at your trial notwithstanding such promise or threat."

The accused did not reply to the magistrate's invitation and caution. Magistrate MacDonald committed Joey to trial on the following count:

"That Joseph Gabriel MacDonald on the 10th day of July 1951 at or near Chepstow in Kings County in the said Province did unlawfully assault Mary Estelle MacKinnon, a woman not his wife, with intent to have carnal knowledge of her without her consent thereby attempting to commit rape contrary to the Criminal Code."

Because of subsequent events, the matter did not proceed to trial.

CHAPTER 4

ROSARY INTERRUPTED

ONE OF MY EARLIEST memories is seeing my father, George MacAulay, standing near the top of the stairs leading to the second storey of our farmhouse. It was early in the morning of November 9, 1951 and he said "Mary Ann died last night". Late the previous night, his neighbour, Alfie MacDonald (who was known as 'Alfie Ade' because his father was Ade MacDonald) had been visiting his then girlfriend Louise Power (whose older sister Florence Celeste 'Esta' Power is my mother) in Little Harbour and he heard some details of Mary Ann's death from one of her neighbours, Roddy Johnson. Alfie hurried from Little Harbour to St. Catherines on foot to inform Mary Ann's brother, George, and his family. My sister Lorraine and her then fiancé, Mark Gillan, were visiting her parents George and Esta MacAulay. Alfie first encountered Lorraine, who was sleeping on the couch in the kitchen because Mark was in the spare bedroom, and he told Lorraine that Mary Ann had been shot and was dead. In a moment of misbelief, Lorraine stated "Alfie, you are drunk" and he replied "I wish it was that simple". Lorraine awakened her father who immediately drove to the MacKinnon residence.

No doubt, the single sentence was calculated to minimize the situation and not unduly upset his children. But, in subsequent years, I also realized that those five words were both non-judgmental and enormously forgiving. Over the years I noted and admired the extraordinary forgiveness that Mary Ann's brothers showed toward the MacDonald family. In discussions of the events, especially the outcome of the murder trial, my father would point out that Joey MacDonald came from a good family. My father fished lobsters adjacent to Joey's older brother, Anselm MacDonald, for about four decades and interacted regularly with him in social settings and community events. Their wives, Esta MacAulay and Emma MacDonald, also interacted socially and served their communities as members of the PEI Women's Institute and the Catholic Women's League. Mary Ann's brother, Joe MacAulay, provided the classic statement on the issue when he said: "There is no sin too big to be forgiven". While Mary Ann's brothers likely chose forgiveness over harbouring grudges for sound moral reasons, it was probably also a better choice for psychological health reasons as well. A recognition that past events cannot be changed and working toward making the future as good as it can be is usually more conducive to good psychological health than harbouring lingering grudges against people you are likely to encounter in your regular activities.

The attempted rape matter was scheduled for trial at Georgetown, PEI on November 13, 1951. Sheriff J.B. Edwin Reid, Sheriff for Kings County, arrived at Mary Ann MacKinnon's residence shortly after 8:00 PM on November 8 to serve a subpoena to have her testify at the trial. The sheriff also had a subpoena for Estelle's former landlady, Mrs. MacLean, in Kingsboro and Mary Ann accompanied the sheriff to Kingsboro because she wanted to make arrangements to have Mrs. MacLean transport her to and from the trial because Mary Ann had no other means of transportation. Sheriff Reid dropped Mary Ann off at her home about 9:00 PM. Sheriff Reid noted that they had encountered heavy rain on the return trip from Kingsboro with the rain subsiding about 9:00 PM.

The MacKinnon farmyard, circa 1950.

While Mary Ann was travelling with Sheriff Reid, itinerant labourer Michael Francis MacDonald arrived at her home. Francis Davey, as he was known (His father was named Jack, his grandfather was named Davey, so most people knew the father as 'Jack Davey' and Francis and his siblings were all referred to as if their surname was 'Davey'.), worked as an agricultural labourer and woodsman wherever he could find work. Sometimes he would stay with the family where he was temporarily employed. He had been cutting pulpwood with Mary Ann's oldest son, Obie, and arrived with the intention of staying for a few days and completing the project. When Mary Ann returned, her younger children were upstairs sleeping and the family discussed listening to a radio program called *Suspense* which aired at 10:00 PM. They checked the radio and found the batteries were weak. Mary Ann's daughter, Alice, offered to go out to an outbuilding they referred to as the 'dairy' to get a better battery.

While in the dairy, Alice heard what sounded like an animal scraping against the building and got scared and returned to the house without the battery. Fearing ridicule, Alice did not report having heard unidentified sounds. Shortly after 9:30 PM, Mary Ann suggested that they say the Rosary before the radio broadcast. Three of her children, Obie, Alice, and Danny, and Francis Davey knelt throughout the kitchen and Mary Ann led the Rosary while sitting on an organ stool. The room was illuminated by an Aladdin lamp and a smaller lamp. The Aladdin lamp used a beehive-shaped mantel and it produced more illumination than the regular lamp which used a wick. Both lamps were fuelled by kerosene.

About hallway through the Rosary, they heard glass breaking and first thought it was the chimney of the Aladdin lamp. Immediately when the sound was heard, Mary Ann swayed on her seat and fell backward. Her family members saw blood coming from behind her left ear and they then realized she had been shot. Her children became scared and Obie moved her into the area at the entrance to the kitchen to protect her from any potential additional shots. On seeing the blood, Francis Davey became sick and went upstairs. After some discussion, Obie decided to stay with his mother while Alice and Danny went to the nearest neighbour's farm which was approximately ¼ mile west of the MacKinnon farm. The neighbours, the Johnsons, did not have a telephone and the nearest telephone was approximately ¾ mile further west at Septimus 'Sept' MacPhee's farm. Sept called Dr. Edward Kassner in Souris who contacted the Souris Detachment of the RCMP at about 10:30 PM.

Shortly after midnight, Coroner Dr. M.N. Beck arrived at the scene and swore in a coroner's jury. The jurors viewed the body and the coroner directed their attention to an entrance wound ½ inch below Mary Ann's left ear lobe. A neighbouring farmer testified and identified the deceased. The jurors viewed the scene and observed that the hole in the screen and the broken window pane aligned with Mary Ann's head as she sat on the organ stool. The coroner adjourned the proceedings.

The jury re-convened at 7:30 PM on November 16, 1951 in the court room in Souris, PEI. The Deputy Attorney General acted for the Crown and called Provincial Pathologist Dr. H.L. Shaw who had done the autopsy. Dr. Shaw testified that he had found a ¼ inch hole ½ inch below the lower tip of the deceased's left ear. The projectile made a hole 10° downward and 5° back and was found lodged in flesh one inch below and one inch behind the deceased's right ear. The pathologist stated that the cause of death was sudden massive hemorrhage from the bullet entering her head and that she was otherwise a perfectly healthy woman. The coroner called several family members and the itinerant labourer who provided details of the events immediately prior to Mary Ann's death.

The coroner then called Dr. Edward Kassner, a family medicine practitioner in Souris, PEI, who described his attendance at the scene with the police and expressed agreement with the pathologist's opinion on the cause of death. The coroner addressed the jury and informed them that there was a person in custody for the murder and that he considered there was sufficient evidence for an open verdict. The jury agreed and brought in the following verdict:

CANADA
PROVINCE OF PRINCE EDWARD ISLAND
COUNTY OF KINGS

An inquisition taken for our Sovereign Lord the King at Souris in Kings County in the said Province on the sixteenth day of November A.D. 1951 before M.N. BECK, M.D. Esquire. One of the Coroners of our said Lord the King for the said County on view of the body of Mary Anne (Mrs. John C.) MacKINNON then and there lying dead upon the oath of:

Kenneth Augustine FRASER

Harold James BRENNAN

Bruce Lowell STEWART

Joseph Arthur PETERS

William Walter DOUGLAS

Ernest Sterling DINGWELL

Leith Irwin DINGWELL

good and lawful men of the said County, duly chosen and who then and there duly sworn, and charged to inquire for our said Lord the King, when, where, how and by what means the said Mary Anne (Mrs. John C.) MacKinnon came to her death do upon this oath say; That Mary Anne (Mrs. John C.) MacKinnon came to her death on November 8th 1951, between the hours of 9:00 PM and 10:30 PM at her home in Little Harbour, Prince Edward Island by being hit by a bullet discharged outside the window by a person or persons unknown. Each of the jurors signed the verdict.

November 9, 1951 was an exciting day for Islanders as Their Royal Highnesses Princess Elizabeth and her husband, Prince Philip the Duke of Edinburgh, were making their first visit to the province. The Royal Train crossed the Northumberland Strait on the world's largest ice-breaking car ferry Canadian National Railway's M.V. *Abegweit. The Guardian of the Gulf* reported that His Royal Highness, a former Lieutenant in the Royal Navy who served on destroyers in Sicily and Japan during World War II, "... made a complete inspection of the powerful and commodious car ferry". He visited the engine room, the bridge, and watched the docking maneuvers from the stern. The Royal Train was then pulled by three 600-horsepower diesel locomotives to Charlottetown where the Royal Couple were met by Premier J. Walter Jones at the Provincial Building, were met at Charlottetown City Hall by Acting Mayor J.D. Stewart, had lunch at Government House with Lieutenant Governor T.W.L. Prowse, toured the Dominion Experimental Farm, took in the first period of the Maritime Major Hockey League game between the Charlottetown Islanders and Moncton Hawks, and attended a state dinner at the Charlottetown Hotel. The province presented Princess Elizabeth with a fox cape made from extra light pearl platinum fox pelts from PEI fox ranches. There were only seven such pelts in existence and four were used to make the cape.

In addition to impressing the staff at the Experimental Farm with her knowledge of the Yorkshire pigs and dairy cattle at the farm, she showed a deep interest in the display of live foxes and mink as well as the exhibit of various colours of fox and mink pelts. She asked if any of the fox pelts were the same as those in her cape and learned that some were similar but none were identical. She also learned that the mink pelts in the coat she received as a wedding gift from Canada were from wild mink rather than ranched mink.

Their Royal Highnesses were warmly greeted by thousands in Charlottetown. But two children who had looked forward to the Royal Visit and their first train travel were not there. Mary Ann's nephew, Gerald MacAulay, and his sister Jean, had been selected to attend as representatives of their classes at Souris High School and St. Mary's Convent. They were scheduled to travel by train from Souris to Charlottetown for the Royal Visit. Their older sister, Lorraine, told them that Mary Ann had died and they would not be going to see the Royal Couple with their classmates. When the high school principal, E. James

MacDonald, noted the absence of both a brother and sister he realized there was something seriously wrong but did not know the reason until later.

The Royal Visit had another impact on the family's activities that day. Helen Morrison grew up in Little Harbour but moved to Washington, D.C. where she increased her standard of living significantly. She returned to PEI every summer and stayed with her brother, Syl, in more modest accommodations than she had become accustomed to. Helen always arrived in a current model luxury car such as a Pontiac Bonneville. She always visited the MacKinnon family and was particularly benevolent to Mary Ann after her husband died. In the summer of 1951, Helen brought Mary Ann a short-sleeved taffeta dress from Washington. Taffeta was regarded as a high-end fabric that was mainly used for ballroom and wedding gowns. Mary Ann really loved the dress. It was royal blue with pink umbrellas. Her family brought it to Dingwell Funeral Home to be used for the wake and funeral. The Dingwell family operated a funeral home in Souris from 1912 to 2017 and, at the time, two Dingwell brothers were the current principals. Both were quite 'proper' in their tastes and regarded Mary Ann's favourite dress to be inappropriate as a burial garment. Finding a suitable dress presented a challenge that day because all the businesses in Charlottetown were closed because of the Royal Visit. Fortunately, Lorraine MacAulay knew an employee of a lady's wear store in Charlottetown who kindly opened the store for Lorraine who purchased a long-sleeved dress that received the undertakers' approval.

Mary Ann died on the second anniversary of her husband's death; J.C. MacKinnon had died on November 8,

1949. She was also buried on the second anniversary of J.C.'s burial. It was Remembrance Day with World War II having ended only six years earlier. The funeral time conflicted with the annual Remembrance Day services, on the morning of November 11, 1951. Despite that, an estimated 250 vehicles travelled the dirt road that is now known as MacKinnon Point Road and the gravel road that is now known as Route 16 from the MacKinnon home to St. Mary's Church in Souris. There was an estimated crowd of 800 at the church which could not accommodate all who had arrived for the Requiem Mass.

Cpl. Strong, who had investigated the complaint that Joey MacDonald had attempted to rape Estelle MacKinnon, arrived at the scene at about 10:30 PM on November 5, shortly after having been contacted by Dr. Kassner. In his report of the event, Cpl. Strong stated that Mary Ann had expressed her fear of Joey both before and after he was granted bail on the attempted rape charge. He also noted that Mary Ann told him that Estelle had similar fears. Joey became the immediate and only suspect in Mary Ann's murder. Cpl. Strong met with Deputy Attorney General Campbell who told him that Joey's bail on the rape charge was cancelled and he instructed him to arrest Joey immediately and bring him to the Souris Detachment. Cpl. Strong and Cst. Ralph Sandberg went to Aeneas MacDonald's farm at approximately 2:30 AM of November 9, 1951 and woke up Aeneas and asked if Joey was home. Aeneas stated he had gone to bed at about 9:00 PM and Joey was not home at that time. But he believed Joey was now home stating that "if he is at home, he'll be up in his bedroom". The policemen arrested Joey in his bedroom and noted that the clothes he had been wearing were on the floor by his bed. They observed that the clothing was generally wet except the bottom of the pant legs which indicated they were protected by boots of the type Joey was known to wear. They seized the wet clothing and, while passing through the porch, they observed a pair of rubber boots with the tops folded down. There were wet spots on the boots and the tops were quite wet and appeared to have been recently worn. Joey admitted that they were his boots and they were the ones he usually wore. Joey was taken to the Souris Detachment and held in custody.

Cpl. Strong then returned to the scene and met with Sgt. D.A. Dunlop of the Charlottetown Criminal Investigation Branch of the RCMP. Sgt. Dunlop had located a single footprint near a corner of the dairy with the toe pointing toward the kitchen window of the MacKinnon house. This indicated that the shooter had been standing with his back to the dairy and viewing the people in the house through the kitchen window using the building as cover. No other footprints were located that night. Two other RCMP members protected the scene for further forensic analysis during daylight and the two NCOs returned to Souris Detachment where they met the Deputy Attorney General who directed Sgt. Dunlop to give the standard warning (that any response would be receivable in evidence) to Joseph Gabriel MacDonald and to charge him with the murder of Mary Ann MacKinnon. Sgt. Dunlop administered the warning but Joey did not respond. He was then taken to the Kings County Jail in Georgetown.

On the morning of November 9, 1951, Cst. T.J. Hogarth and Police Service Dog 'King' arrived on PEI by air from

Moncton, New Brunswick. PSD King was able to locate a track approximately ⅓ of a mile west of the scene. The track led down a steep bank to the water's edge and back up the bank but the dog lost the track approximately 300 yards from Joey's residence.

The investigators also examined the scene that morning in an effort to determine where the fatal shot originated. The ground slopes downward on the north side of the MacKinnon house and the bullet penetrated a screen and the glass in a window on the north side of the house. The next closest point with a parallel elevation is approximately ¾ of a mile away. The investigators concluded that the shot must have been fired within 20 feet of the window otherwise the shooter would not have been able to align the weapon with the target. Even at this distance, it was a feat of incredible marksmanship given that the shot was taken in darkness, the weapon had non-illuminated open sights, the butt (which would normally be pressed against the shooter's shoulder to hold the weapon steady) had been sawn off, the shot was through a screen and a small pane of glass, the target was illuminated only by the light of two kerosene lamps, and the shot, though of small calibre, hit a very vulnerable region which proved to be almost instantly fatal.

On November 19, 1951 the RCMP executed a search warrant at Aeneas MacDonald's farm and located a Cooey Sure-Shot, bolt action, .22 calibre, repeater rifle, 24-inch barrel, with no serial number and one live round in the breech as well as two live rounds in the magazine. The rifle was in a concealed position behind a folding garage door. The stock of the weapon had been sawn off to pistol length and it smelled like it had been recently fired. No finger-prints were found on the rifle but the front sight had mud and what appeared to be a long black horse hair on it. The rifle, the unexpended rounds, and the lead that the pathologist recovered from Mary Ann's head were forwarded to the RCMP Crime Detection Laboratory in Ottawa, Ontario. A search of the scene, using mine detection equipment and the police dog, did not locate any spent cartridges. The mine detector was also used where the tracks had led to the beach but nothing was found.

On November 15, 1951 Cpl. Strong received information that Luke Francis Melchaides 'Shady' Power had seen horse tracks over his recently plowed land. 'Shady Power' would be a great name for a fictional fraudster but the actual Shady Power was born on December 10, which is the feast day of Saint Melchaides, and his nickname comes from his third given name and not any propensity to be involved in dubious business practices. Shady's business ethics were more aligned with the canonized pope he was named after than those of a character with the ability to increase the demand for ten-foot poles. Mrs. Wiggs, in her references to him, always referred to him as Melchaides Power. Shady and his father, William F. Power, farmed in Little Harbour. Their farm was located between the MacKinnon and Aeneas MacDonald farms. He was related by marriage to both sides of this story – his older sister, Esta, was married to Mary Ann's brother George and his younger brother, Dickie, was married to Joey's older sister Mary Ellen. Shady reported seeing horse tracks across land that he had plowed on November 8 on the morning of November 9. The tracks were in both directions – going in the direction of the MacKinnon farm and also leaving the direction of the MacKinnon farm. A few days later (possibly November 14 to the best of his recollection), Shady noticed that some of his fences and those of a neighbour had been cut and the horse tracks led through the cuts. Cpl. Strong examined the cuts, noting they were in obscure locations, and took some samples of the wire. He also located an area where it appeared that a horse had been tied. There were two relatively recent deposits of horse manure, a piece of tarred rope was found beside a tree, and there was considerable tramping of the ground consistent with the presence of a horse for a period of time.

The following day, Cpl. Strong executed another search warrant at the Aeneas MacDonald farm and recovered a pair of pliers with wire cutting capability from the tool box of a Fordson tractor that was stored in the garage where the rifle had been located earlier.

On November 20, 1951, S/Sgt. William Wallace Sutherland of the RCMP Crime Detection Laboratory in Ottawa reported having identified the likely manufacturer of the bullet that the pathologist recovered at the autopsy and having fired similar test bullets from the rifle seized from Aeneas MacDonald's garage. The insides of rifle barrels are 'rifled'; that is, they have spiral grooves that make the projectile spin for greater accuracy. The grooves impart marks on the exiting projectiles which are unique to each weapon. S/Sgt. Sutherland microscopically compared the recovered bullet to the bullets used in test firing the weapon. He looked for markings on the test fired projectiles that were also present on the bullet recovered at the autopsy. The firearms expert expressed the opinion that the recovered bullet was fired from a rifle which was rifled to the same specifications as the seized weapon and that it was very probably fired from the seized weapon.

In a report dated December 15, 1951, S/Sgt. Sutherland reported that the pieces of wire that had been submitted for examination and comparison to the pliers seized from the tool box in Aeneas MacDonald's tractor were broken by repeated bending and twisting actions and were not cut. S/Sgt. Sutherland concluded that the wire had been held by a tool and repeatedly flexed or twisted near where the tool was placed causing the wires to break. He made impressions on test pieces of similar wire with the seized pliers that were consistent with the impressions that were on the wires that had been seized from the fences near where Shady Power had been plowing. S/Sgt. Sutherland then examined the tool markings on the seized wires and the test wires microscopically but did not identify any corresponding characteristics that were significant enough to positively state that the seized pliers were used to break the wires in the fences near the plowed field.

This evidence would be entered at the preliminary hearing and the murder trial the following year.

CHAPTER 5
RIFLE DETAILS REVEALED

THE PRELIMINARY HEARING in the murder case began in Georgetown, PEI on December 7, 1951 before Stipendiary Magistrate Joseph W. MacDonald, KC. Deputy Attorney General J.O.C. Campbell, KC again represented the Crown with H. Frank MacPhee, KC and James B. Johnston, KC representing the accused.

The proceedings took place in what is now a provincially designated historic place. The Kings County Court House is a one and a half storey Romanesque Revival style building with an exterior made of red PEI sandstone and grey Wallace sandstone from Nova Scotia. It is one of the great public buildings designed by renowned architect William Critchlow Harris, RCA. The cornerstone was laid on July 20, 1887 to commemorate Queen Victoria's Golden Jubilee.

Kings County Court House,
Georgetown, PEI.

Provincial Pathologist, Dr. Harold Shaw, testified that he performed an autopsy on Mary Ann MacKinnon and stated the cause of death was a lead missile entering her head about one-half inch below the tip of her left ear, travelling through the spinal canal without severing the spinal cord, and lodging in the right side of her neck. Dr. Shaw placed the piece of lead in a locked cabinet and turned it over to Cst. George Cass of the RCMP.

Cst. Cass testified that he received the bullet from Dr. Shaw on November 10, 1951, placed it in a small bottle and secured it in a cupboard at Souris Detachment. The following day he travelled by plane to Ottawa and turned the bullet over to S/Sgt. Sutherland at the RCMP Crime Detection Laboratory in Rockcliffe, Ontario. Cst. Cass also delivered three unspent rounds of ammunition (one recovered from the breech and two from the magazine of the rifle that was seized from Aeneas MacDonald's garage) and the .22 calibre bolt-action rifle.

S/Sgt. Sutherland gave evidence that he had worked at the Crime Detection Laboratory for four years and had studied firearms and ballistics in Regina, with the New York Police Department, and the Federal Bureau of Investigation in Washington, D.C. S/Sgt. Sutherland said he was familiar with the type of rifle, a Canadian-made Cooey repeater. He testified that he test-fired the weapon and compared the test bullets with the one he received from Cst. Cass. The firearms expert stated that he could say positively that the recovered bullet had been fired from a rifle of the same type as the seized weapon and that it was probably fired from the seized weapon. S/Sgt. Sutherland testified that factory .22 calibre bullets weigh approximately 29 grams; the recovered bullet weighed 24.98 grams, and, in his opinion, likely originally weighed approximately 29 grams. The bullet would have been distorted from its original shape and would also have lost some of its mass as it travelled through the barrel of the rifle and the victim's flesh.

Cst. Thomas Joseph Hogarth testified that he had worked with PSD King, a three-year old German Shepherd which had been trained by the RCMP and had worked on about 50 cases. He had King smell a piece of cloth containing Joey MacDonald's bodily scent provided by Cpl. Strong and circled the MacKinnon house with the dog. PSD King did not locate any matching scent in the vicinity of the house but did detect a matching scent about ¼ of a mile away. The PSD could detect the scent in sheltered areas but lost the scent in open areas. At one point, the scent led to a bank above the shore line. Cst. Hogarth left King at the top of the bank, descended to the water's edge but did not detect anything of interest. The dog then followed the scent in the direction of the accused's residence but lost the scent again.

Dr. Edward Kassner gave evidence of the time he attended at the scene and agreed with Dr. Shaw' opinion on the cause of death.

Sheriff Edwin B. Reid testified that he had four subpoenas to serve on November 8, 1951 including one for Mary Ann and another for Mrs. MacLean in Kingsboro. Sheriff Reid testified about driving Mary Ann to and from Kingsboro on the night of her death.

Michael Francis MacDonald (more commonly known as Francis Davey) testified that he arrived at the MacKinnon home after dark on November 8, 1951. He was there to make arrangements with Obie MacKinnon to cut some pulpwood the following day. Mary Ann was not home when he arrived but she returned later with Sheriff Reid. Some of the MacKinnon children were in bed but Obie, Alice, and Danny were in the kitchen. He testified that the family wanted to listen to a radio program but the batteries were running low and Alice went outside to get a better battery. He described the layout of the kitchen and the positions the family members were in when they were saying the Rosary. He described hearing the sound of glass breaking and thought it was a lamp globe but he saw Mary Ann fall backwards. Seeing blood, he got weak and went upstairs to lie down. He also described seeing the broken window and the hole in the screen. Mr. MacDonald testified that he knew Joey MacDonald and had worked with him one afternoon at Dickie Power's farm.

Dickie Power is the accused's brother-in-law. He also stated that he had left PEI around the end of lobster season [The lobster season in the area starts on May 1 and ends on June 30.] to work in the woods in Nova Scotia and had returned to PEI about the end of August. He saw Joey MacDonald near the Matthew and MacLean Store in Souris and Joey asked Francis if he had heard about "the racket" he had gotten into and mentioned the rape charge and that Mary Ann had him charged. He stated that Joey threatened Mary Ann by stating: "I'll get that old son of a whore, I'll shoot her".

Alice MacKinnon corroborated Francis MacDonald's description of the setting and also testified about going out to get a better battery for the radio. She testified about being scared by hearing a scraping sound on the outside of the dairy and returning to the house without a battery. She did not mention hearing the scraping sound to her family because she was afraid they would make fun of her.

Obie MacKinnon testified that his older sister, Estelle, had been away studying nursing but returned home following her mother's death. He also testified about observing strange horse hoof prints on the farm after his mother's funeral. The prints were not made by the horse that was on the MacKinnon farm because their mare was shod and the tracks were that of an unshod horse.

Danny MacKinnon testified that, after his mother's death, he and Alice went to Mrs. Mary Mossey's residence for help. Mary (Mrs. Peter) Mossey testified that she lived about a quarter of a mile from the MacKinnon home and had known Mary Ann for years and saw her almost every day. Mrs. Mossey testified that she saw a car travelling in the direction of the MacKinnon house a few minutes before 9:00 PM on November 8, 1951. At about 10:00 PM the same night, Alice and Danny MacKinnon arrived at her house. They were crying, and they said their mother had been killed. Mrs. Mossey said she went to the MacKinnon house with the children.

Estelle MacKinnon testified that Joey MacDonald had shown her what appeared to be the handle of a revolver at her boarding house in Kingsboro in May 1951. She also testified about him threatening the Mounties, or anyone that got in his road, while he was making moonshine. Estelle stated that Joey was very upset about the breakdown of their relationship and stated he would use the gun on himself or someone else. She also told the court that Joey

had a history of conflict with her mother who did not approve of Joey dating Estelle. Mary Ann regarded her oldest
daughter as a glamorous young lady who was destined to
marry above her current social class.

Joey's lawyer objected. He said Estelle's evidence should
not be admitted because it was irrelevant and showed the
defendant to be of bad character. Magistrate MacDonald
agreed. He allowed only the evidence about Estelle's age
and occupation, leaving her nursing training and returning home after her mother's death, and that she knew the
accused.

Cst. Ralph D. Sandberg of the Souris Detachment of
the RCMP testified about attending the scene with Cpl.
Strong and Dr. Kassner and finding Mary Ann dead on
the floor. Cst. Sandberg testified that he went to Aeneas
MacDonald's house with Cpl. Strong and they seized some
wet clothing and a pair of hip rubber boots. He testified
that, on November 10, 1951, he and Cpl. Strong executed
a search warrant at Aeneas MacDonald's farm and they
seized a .22 calibre rifle with the breech closed, mud on
the front sight, and some mud in the muzzle.

The mud was dry but not caked. The breech smelled
like it had been recently fired and there was a piece of
horse hair on the front sight. There were three bullets in
the weapon but one was placed backwards. He turned the
rifle and the ammunition over to Cst. George Cass. Cst.
Sandberg testified that he searched the area of the
MacKinnon home for several days and found some footprints near the dairy and some about 300 yards southeast
of the house. He also found some horse's tracks and located a place where it appeared that a horse had been tied

with some comparatively fresh horse droppings. He also located a piece of rope about eight or nine feet long and a dirty white handkerchief that had been folded crosswise with two knots tied, one in each corner.

Cst. Sandberg also testified that the ground slopes decidedly downward on the north side of the MacKinnon house toward a bank and a bog with water in it. The road about a mile away was level with the kitchen window but he expressed the view that a .22 calibre bullet would not be fatal from that distance. Cst. Sandburg lined the holes in the screen and the pane of glass that the bullet travelled through and found the hole in the glass was slightly higher than the hole in the screen outside of it. He stated that a line drawn from the hole in the glass and through the screen would extend on a slightly downward angle to a spot on a tree 18 or 20 feet from the outside of the window. That spot would be about the height of a man.

Cst. Sandberg also testified that, on November 15, 1951, he learned some fences in the area had been cut and that he searched Aeneas MacDonald's premises again and seized a pair of pliers. He also took some samples of horsehair from MacDonald's horse. He forwarded the seized samples of horsehair and the horsehair that he recovered at the place where a horse had been tied on the MacKinnon farm to the Crime Detection Laboratory in Regina, Saskatchewan.

The last witness on the first day of the preliminary hearing was local undertaker E. Sterling Dingwell. He testified to removing Mary Ann's body from the scene and delivering it to the provincial pathologist and identifying it to the pathologist.

The preliminary hearing resumed on December 14, 1951. Shady Power testified that he plowed two fields on the back of his property (which is situated between the MacKinnon and the MacDonald farms) during the week prior to the murder and on the two days after the murder. Shady testified that on November 9 he noticed some horse tracks across a field that he had plowed the previous day. He also testified that the tracks were not there in the evening of November 8 when he finished plowing which is indicative of a horse having crossed the newly plowed land overnight on November 8-9.

Glynn Stewart, a carpenter, testified that he removed the window and screen on the north kitchen window of the MacKinnon residence at the request of the police. He stated that he secured the screen, which was unframed, to maintain its original alignment with the glass the bullet had passed through.

Cpl. Allen M. Johnston, an RCMP identification specialist stationed in Charlottetown, testified about the measurements he had taken at the crime scene. He provided and elaborated upon a number of photographs he had taken at the scene. He also entered as exhibits plaster casts of a footprint he located near the dairy and three footprints he located south of the house in a strawberry bed, and four more footprints he located about a mile from the MacKinnon property.

The preliminary hearing was originally adjourned until December 20, 1951 but there was no evidence presented that date. It resumed on January 10, 1952 with cross-examination of Cpl. Johnston. Cpl. Johnston testified that the footprints that were the subjects of the plaster casts were probably made by the boots that were seized at the time of Joey MacDonald's arrest, early on November 9, 1951.

The Crown called its last witness – Cpl. Lionel F.M. Strong who was in charge of the Souris Detachment of the RCMP. Cpl. Strong testified about the motive for the murder with defence counsel objecting to references to the rape charge and any evidence that could be categorized as hearsay. Magistrate MacDonald ruled that Cpl. Strong could refer to the July 10, 1951 events provided that he did not use the word 'rape'. Cpl. Strong also testified about having been called to the MacKinnon residence on June 30, 1951 because Joey MacDonald was there, and, when told that Estelle MacKinnon no longer wanted to keep him company, he had caused a disturbance.

Cpl. Strong testified about arresting Joey MacDonald, seizing his clothing and rubber boots, and executing search warrants where a rifle, pliers and horse hair were seized from his father's premises. Cpl. Strong also testified about following horse tracks from the MacDonald farm to the scene of the murder.

Following submissions by counsel for the Crown and the accused, Magistrate MacDonald committed Joseph Gabriel MacDonald to stand trial for murder at the next sitting of the Supreme Court of Prince Edward Island in July 1952.

CHAPTER 6
VERDICT RENDERED

THE MURDER TRIAL proceedings began on July 8, 1952 with the same counsel representing both the Crown and the accused. The only change was their post-nominals which had changed since the preliminary hearing concluded. On February 6, 1952, King George VI died and Queen Elizabeth II ascended to the Throne. With the change in the monarchy, counsel's post-nominals changed from KC (King's Counsel) to QC (Queen's Counsel).

Deputy Attorney General Campbell presented the case to a grand jury made up of twelve men from Kings County: Cameron Reid (foreman), Daniel McIntyre, Lorne Johnson, Felix Peters, Ray Farquharson, Louis Jenkins, Daniel MacRae, John MacLeod, Glen Johnson, George MacPherson, John Bruce, and Walter Burdett.

In the Supreme Court of Judicature Court of Assize Jail Delivery, begun and holden at Georgetown within and for Kings County, in the Province of Prince Edward Island, in the Dominion of Canada, on the second Tuesday in July in the first year of the Reign of our Sovereign Lady Elizabeth the Second, by the Grace of God of Great Britain, Ireland, and the British Dominions beyond the Seas, QUEEN, Defender of the Faith; and in the year of our Lord one thousand nine hundred and fifty-two.

The Jurors for Our Lady the Queen, upon their oath, present that Joseph Gabriel MacDonald murdered Mary Anne (Mrs. John C.) MacKinnon at Little Harbour in Kings County aforesaid on the eighth day of November, 1951.

Joey was arraigned on the charge before Chief Justice Thane A. Campbell and a petit jury in the Kings County Court House in Georgetown, PEI on July 9, 1952 and he pleaded 'not guilty'. The same counsel represented the Crown and the accused that had represented the parties at the preliminary hearing. The jury consisting of: Elijah Pierce (foreman); Frederick MacKenzie; Charles J. Fraser; John M. Farrell; Thomas McCluskey; Joseph McCormack; Charles Campbell; Peter Conway; Daniel McLean; Walter Shaw; George MacPherson; and Joseph Morrison; was selected from an array of 68 prospective jurors.

Grand juries were a relic of colonial times. Grand juries in England can be traced back to the Assize of Clarendon in 1164. Originally, grand juries were local inhabitants who had a duty to report all the crimes they suspected of having been committed and draw up bills of indictment against those suspected of crimes. The system evolved to the grand juries being composed of persons with no first-hand knowledge of the alleged crimes hearing witnesses to the events and deciding whether or not to indict the person(s) accused of the crime(s). The grand jury system became part of Canadian criminal procedure as the provinces and territories enacted legislation with respect to juries. Although the enactment of criminal law and criminal procedure is constitutionally reserved to Parliament

For use of Prothonotary :

Proceedings :

Grand Jury return *True* Bill

Date *8 July, 1952*

Plea : *Not Guilty*

Date *8 July, 1952*

Ready for trial : *any time*

Trial :

Date *July 9, 10, 11, 12.*

Verdict : *We find that the
accused, who struck
Mary Ann MacDonald was
insane at the time of the
commission of the offence and
we declare, that the accused
him of the said offence on
account of such insanity*

Date — *13 July, 1952.*

Sentence :

Date

Supreme Court

Kings   County

July   Sittings, 19 52

The ~~King~~ Queen

vs.

JOSEPH GABRIEL MacDONALD

Indictment

Charge : Murder

Crown Witnesses ;
1A. Valerius MacDonald.
1. Dr. Harold Shaw.

~~Crown Witnesses:~~
2. Constable George Cass.

3. S/Sgt. William Wallace Sutherland.

4. S/Sgt. James Robinson.

5. Dr. Edward Kassner.

6. Sheriff Edwin Reid.

7. Michael Francis MacDonald.

8. Alice Pauline MacKinnon.

9. Alban MacKinnon.

10. Daniel MacKinnon.

11. Mary (Mrs.Peter) Mossey.

12. Mary Estelle MacKinnon.

13. Const. Ralph E. Sandberg.

14. E. Sterling Dingwell.

15. Luke Powers.

16. Glynneth Stewart.

17. Cpl. Allen M. Johnston.

18. Cpl. Lionel F.M. Strong.

19. Const. Arthur P. Tomilson.

Write "True Bill" or "No Bill"
as the case may be.   For self and fellows,

Foreman, Grand Jury
For self and fellows.

Verdict Rendered

In the Supreme Court of Judicature

CANADA
Province of Prince Edward Island
KINGS COUNTY

Court of Assize and General Jail Delivery, begun and holden at Georgetown within and for Kings County, in the Province of Prince Edward Island, in the Dominion of Canada, on the second Tuesday in July in the first year of the Reign of our Sovereign ~~Lord~~ Lady Elizabeth the second ~~George the Sixth~~, by the Grace of God of Great Britain, Ireland, and the British Dominions beyond the Seas, ~~KING~~, Defender of the Faith, ~~Emperor of India~~; and in the year of our Lord one thousand nine hundred and fifty-two

The Jurors for our ~~Lord the King~~ Lady the Queen, upon their oath, present that Joseph Gabriel MacDonald murdered Mary Anne (Mrs. John C.) MacKinnon at Little Harbour in Kings County aforesaid on the eighth day of November, 1951.

Attorney General
pro. Dom. Reg.

69

under Head 91(27) of the *Constitution* Act, 1867, provinces have jurisdiction over the administration of justice in the province including the constitution of provincial courts, both criminal and civil, pursuant to Head 92(14) of the *Constitution* Act, 1867. Provinces enacted legislation giving grand juries jurisdiction to indict persons alleged to have committed indictable offences. The legislation typically outlined the qualifications of the jurors (usually male property owners), the number of jurors (twelve in PEI at the relevant time), and the plurality required for a verdict (usually a majority if the jury had fewer than thirteen members). Grand jury proceedings were conducted *ex parte* (the accused was not present either in person or by counsel) and strict rules of evidence (such as exclusion of hearsay evidence) were not rigidly adhered to. Grand juries were required to return a 'true bill' if they were satisfied that the accused should stand trial and a 'no bill' if they found inadequate evidence to put the accused on his/her defence. 'No bill' decisions were quite rare as grand jury proceedings followed the accused having already been committed to trial following a preliminary hearing or having waived his/her right to a preliminary hearing, juries only heard the Crown's version of the evidence, the rules of evidence were relaxed, only a majority (not unanimity as prevailed in petit juries) was required, and the test for indictment was relatively low. By the early 1970s, most Canadian jurisdictions had amended their jury legislation to abolish grand juries. During the grand jury era, juries selected for individual trials (both civil and criminal) were referred to as petit juries and today they are simply referred to as juries.

Grand juries were usually empaneled at the beginning of sessions of superior courts of criminal jurisdiction and, in some jurisdictions, had other tasks. In this case, the grand jury inspected the county jail and the court house and found them to be in good repair except that the flue in the jail needed to be extended to prevent the kitchen range from smoking and spoiling the paint. They also recommended that the floor in the main entrance be covered with battleship linoleum.

In the criminal matter before them, they brought down a 'true bill' in the following format:

In the Supreme Court of Judicature Court of Assize Jail Delivery, begun and holden at Georgetown within and for Kings County, in the Province of Prince Edward Island, in the Dominion of Canada, on the second Tuesday in July in the first year of the Reign of our Sovereign Lady Elizabeth the Second, by the Grace of God of Great Britain, Ireland, and the British Dominions beyond the Seas, QUEEN, Defender of the Faith; and in the year of our Lord one thousand nine hundred and fifty-two.

The Jurors for Our Lady the Queen, upon their oath, present that Joseph Gabriel MacDonald murdered Mary Anne (Mrs. John C.) MacKinnon at Little Harbour in Kings County aforesaid on the eighth day of November, 1951.

The Deputy Attorney General gave an opening address in which he attempted to enunciate the accused's state of mind to show his motivation to commit murder.
Mr. MacPhee strenuously objected to any introduction of evidence that was more related to the rape charge than the murder charge or which attacked the character of the accused. The Crown intended to call Estelle MacKinnon early in the trial to establish the motivation for the offence. Defence counsel suggested that "The Crown will put on an attractive witness who will tell a pathetic story" to develop emotional stress early in the proceedings and have an adverse effect on the jurors.

Crown counsel outlined the relationship between Estelle and Joey, including early meetings when he gave her a drive home from Souris and tried to kiss her. During many dates Joey was often drinking moonshine and pressing her for sexual relations. Crown counsel also said that, on an earlier occasion, Joey had entered her bedroom in a boarding house and showed her a revolver and that he had threatened to use the revolver on himself. Estelle, seeing his state of mind, had agreed to continue dating him until she left for nurse's training in September. She also, in front of her mother, said that she did not want to go out with him again. Crown Counsel also stated that the jury would hear evidence from a witness who had heard the accused make a threat, about a month after the rape charge, to shoot Mary Ann. He concluded by describing the gravity of the crime – a mother being shot while praying the Rosary with her family: "Some mad man fires a bullet, and with an act of faith on her lips a mother is dead," he said.

The Crown called Dr. Harold Shaw, the Provincial Pathologist, who gave the same evidence as he had given at the preliminary hearing.

The Crown then called Estelle MacKinnon who described her relationship with Joey starting with the fact they had attended the one-room Chepstow school together and that they began dating when she obtained a teaching permit. She testified that generally he was drinking moonshine before their dates but sometimes "he was decent and sober", a comment that attracted an objection from defence counsel. The court had the jury temporarily removed from the courtroom and he conducted what is known as a *voir dire* to determine how much, if any, of Estelle's evidence would be admitted. Mr. MacPhee submitted that what Joey had done in 1950 was not relevant to the murder trial and evidence that attacks the general character of an accused is inadmissible. He submitted that using the accused's state of mind to establish a motive for murder was farfetched in this case and he submitted that, in this case, motive should only be established by examining the relationship between the accused and the victim. The Deputy Attorney General submitted that evidence of animosity is admissible, to which Mr. MacPhee expressed agreement but stated that the accused's relationship with Estelle had no bearing on this case. His Lordship ruled that the evidence of relations between Estelle and the accused was admissible to establish animosity between the deceased and accused since May 1951. Estelle described her attempts to break up with Joey and his coming to her bedroom with a revolver "to blow the head of Mounties or anyone else" who obstructed him while he was making moonshine. She also testified that she had told Joey in front of her mother that she did not want to go out with him anymore because of his drinking and that "he was too passionate". Estelle stated that her mother had tried to reason with Joey but he would not listen to her.

In cross-examination, by Mr. MacPhee, Estelle testified that she had told Joey she was not interested in continuing to go out with him several times including one time in the presence of her mother.

The Crown then called Valerius A. MacDonald, the Chief Surveyor of PEI, who introduced a number of maps and charts he had prepared that showed the MacKinnon house and its relationship with the nearby dairy, and an aerial map showing the region.

Cst. Ralph Sandberg of the Souris Detachment of the RCMP gave testimony consistent with his evidence at the preliminary hearing. He elaborated on his evidence with respect to the likely path the fatal bullet followed, from leaving the barrel of the rifle until it struck its intended target. He testified that he lined up the hole in the glass with the hole in the screen and it intersected with a spot in a tree at a point higher than a man standing at the base of the tree. In cross-examination by Mr. Johnston, Cst. Sandberg agreed that Aeneas MacDonald had been cooperative in the several searches of his premises. He also stated the rifle he seized was a low-cost weapon and that it smelled like it had been recently fired. Cst. Sandberg stated that there would be traces of odor from a weapon fired with smokeless powder for approximately a month.

S/Sgt. James Robinson who was in charge of the Hair and Fibre Section of the RCMP Crime Detection

Laboratory in Regina, Saskatchewan testified that the horse hair samples collected from Aeneas MacDonald's horse were similar in every way to the horse hair samples recovered from the site where a horse had apparently been tied on the MacKinnon property and could have come from the same animal.

S/Sgt. William W. Sutherland, who was in charge of the Firearms Section of the RCMP Crime Detection Laboratory in Rockcliffe, Ontario, gave the same evidence he gave at the preliminary hearing. The Crown attempted use S/Sgt Sutherland's testimony to introduce microphotographs of the fatal bullet. Mr. MacPhee objected to the admission of such evidence because the photographs were secondary evidence. The best evidence, the bullet itself, was already in evidence, he said.

Crown Counsel submitted that the courts admit evidence of photographs of fingerprints on surfaces as well as other scientific evidence and that the photos would be helpful to the jury. The court ruled the photographs were admissible to show the steps the expert witness used to arrive at his opinion and to show tiny details not visible to the naked eye. S/Sgt. Sutherland described the instruments he used including the camera equipment and the microscopic comparisons, and the test firing of the suspect weapon. In cross-examination by Mr. MacPhee, S/Sgt. Sutherland agreed that there might be up to 1,200 rifles of the same calibre and with similar manufacturing characteristics as the suspect rifle. The distortion in the fatal bullet made it impossible to state definitively that it was fired from the suspect rifle. When defence counsel suggested that smokeless powder is odourless, the witness stated that a characteristic odour emanates from a recently fired rifle and that odour could be present for approximately 12 hours. Mr. Justice Campbell noted that the rifle had not been examined until approximately 38 hours after MaryAnn was shot.

Michael Francis 'Francis Davey' MacDonald repeated the testimony he gave at the preliminary hearing. That included describing the events in the MacKinnon house on the night of November 8, 1951 and the conversation he had with Joey around the end of August 1951. In that conversation, Joey asked Francis if he had heard about "the racket" Joey had gotten into which led to a discussion about Mary Ann and Joey stating: "I'll get the old son of a whore, I'll shoot her". In cross-examination, Francis stated that he always gets weak at the sight of blood and, after witnessing the fatality; he went upstairs and lied down.

Mr. Hessian did the examination in chief of Mrs. Mary Mossey. She said she lived ten or eleven chains [A chain is a surveyor's unit of measure and is 66 feet; the width of a typical PEI farm is ten chains.]from the Mrs. MacKinnon who the neighbours regarded as "a real nice woman".

She saw a car going to the MacKinnon house but did not see it leave. She went to bed at about 9:30 PM. At about 10:10 PM, Alice and Danny MacKinnon came to her house. They were crying and told her that their mother had been shot. Her son and grandson went to notify a doctor and she took the MacKinnon children back home where Mrs. Mossey saw Mary Ann lying in a pool of blood with no apparent pulse or heartbeat. She remained at the MacKinnon house until approximately 4:00 AM: a doctor and the police arrived while she was there.

Shady Power repeated the testimony he had given at the preliminary hearing about, on the Sunday after the shooting, noticing horse tracks going both ways in the general direction of the MacKinnon property.

Cpl. Allan Johnston of the RCMP Identification Section in Charlottetown testified about photographs and plaster casts of footprints he had taken. He made plaster casts of footprints found near the dairy, in a strawberry patch 318 feet southeast of the MacKinnon house, and in a field south of the buildings on a farm owned by Sept MacPhee. He received both boots that had been seized from the MacDonald house in the early hours of November 9, 1951 from Cpl. Strong and compared them to the plaster casts. Cpl. Johnson found a number of accidental similarities (accidental characteristics on objects are unique marks that were not present on manufacture and which generally result from use of the object which makes them useful to identify individual objects such as tire tracks and footwear) between the accused's boots and the plaster casts of the footprints especially in the area between the ball of the foot and the heel. On the right heel there was a scar present on the boot that was replicated in the plaster casts. Mr. MacPhee strenuously objected to the admission of the photographs and plaster casts but Chief Justice Campbell admitted them. Cpl. Johnston testified that the ground was level for four feet six inches from the MacKinnon house with an abrupt drop over the next two or three feet then a gradual downward slope. Cpl. Johnston testified that he crouched and looked through the hole in the screen from outside and found the hole in the screen to be slightly below and to the east of the hole in the glass.

Sheriff Edwin Reid repeated the testimony he provided at the preliminary hearing noting that, when he drove Mary Ann back to her residence, at approximately 9:00 PM, her health seemed to be perfect.

Alice MacKinnon testified that six of her brothers and sisters were in bed at the time her mother was shot. She repeated the testimony she had given at the preliminary hearing about going out to get a battery for the radio, hearing a brushing sound behind the dairy and returning to the house without the battery and not reporting being scared on the assumption she would be laughed at. Alice also described hearing the glass break, her oldest brother moving her mother to the hall, and going to Mrs. Mossey's house and reporting the event.

Obie MacKinnon, Mary Ann's oldest son, testified that he had come into the house about ten minutes before Sheriff Reid brought his mother home. He reconfirmed the positions of the people present in the kitchen when the shooting occurred. He stated that he moved his mother to the hall and removed her dentures and tried to get her to speak but there was no response. He also stated that he later had observed some strange hoof prints on the farm from an unshod horse. The mare on the MacKinnon farm was shod, he testified.

Danny MacKinnon repeated his testimony from the preliminary hearing about the position of the persons in the kitchen and the events immediately before and after the shooting.

The defence did not call any evidence.

Testimony ended in the afternoon of Saturday, July 12, 1952 and Deputy Attorney General Campbell summed up the Crown's case by describing it as being based on some direct evidence (notably the testimony of Michael Francis MacDonald about the intent to shoot the victim) but largely on circumstantial evidence. Mr. Campbell noted that some circumstantial evidence is more reliable than eye witness evidence which can be fallible. He cited some court decisions that held that circumstantial evidence was acceptable when there are a number of relevant events which lead to a definitive conclusion. The leading decision on convictions based solely on circumstantial, rather than direct, evidence is the 1838 English decision known as *Hodge's Case*. In *Hodge's Case*, Baron Alderson stated the rule that, in a case dependent entirely on circumstantial evidence, before the prisoner could be found guilty the jury must be satisfied "not only that those circumstances were consistent with his having committed the act, but they must also be satisfied that the facts were such as to be inconsistent with any other rational conclusion than the prisoner was the guilty person". Mr. Campbell submitted that the case against Joey consisted of both direct and circumstantial evidence making the *Hodge's Case* precedent inapplicable. Without there having been any medical evidence tendered at the trial, Mr. Campbell raised the possibility that the accused could have been insane at the time of the offence due to consumption of moonshine. As well, there was no evidence tendered that suggested the accused had consumed alcohol before committing the offence. The Crown submitted that the accused's ability to have the requisite *mens rea* [guilty intent] for a murder

conviction could have been diminished by alcohol-induced
insanity, but Mr. Campbell did not address the likely increased physical challenges that would have resulted from
pre-event alcohol consumption. If, as Cst. Sandberg the-
orized, the accused fired the fatal shot from a perch in a
tree eighteen to twenty feet from the window, at a target
inside illuminated only by the light of two kerosene lamps,
from a rifle with open sights and most of the butt removed,
it was an incredible feat of marksmanship for even a completely sober person and it would have been even more
challenging for an intoxicated person. It would be a somewhat difficult task even for a current skilled marksman
with a full-length rifle and a night-vision telescope.

After an adjournment for supper, Mr. MacPhee addressed the jury for over two hours. He attacked the
Crown witnesses, especially the expert evidence given by
the police witnesses. He also pointed out inconsistencies
in the testimony of Crown witnesses and categorized it
as an entirely circumstantial case thus making the rule in
Hodge's Case applicable. Being a circumstantial evidence
case, he told the jury that a conviction required them to
find beyond a reasonable doubt that the evidence must
both be consistent with Joey having murdered Mary Ann
and inconsistent with any other rational conclusion. Mr.
MacPhee submitted that the evidence did not meet this
standard. Interestingly, defence counsel did not comment
on the possible availability of the defence of insanity.

In his charge to the jury, Mr. Justice Campbell summarized the events and the evidence. Since murder was a
capital offence at that time with the only available sentence being "hanged by the neck until dead", he told the

jury that, if they found the accused guilty, they could make
a recommendation for mercy. He complimented the police for their fair and unbiased testimony and particularly
stressed the value of Cpl. Johnston's evidence. He told the
jury that the rules about alcoholic insanity were the same
as those for any other form of insanity and stated that a
person who is found to be insane cannot be convicted of
committing a crime while insane. His Lordship addressed
the possibility that Joey harboured an irrational dislike for
Mary Ann because of her efforts to pursue a rape charge
against him. He informed the jury that the accused must
have the mental capacity to form the intent to commit
murder in order to be convicted.

The jury began deliberations at 10:55 PM on July 12,
1952. When the jury began deliberations, Mr. MacPhee
submitted to the court that the court erred because His
Lordship's remarks regarding the defences available to the
accused amounted to a comment on the accused's failure to testify. He asked Mr. Justice Campbell to recall the
jury and inform them that he erred in making the remarks
and instruct them to completely disregard the remarks.
In Canadian criminal proceedings, the Crown is required
to prove each constituent element of the charge beyond
a reasonable doubt. An accused person is not required to
testify or otherwise provide evidence of his/her inno-
cence. Neither a judge nor a jury is permitted to use an
accused's failure to testify on his/her own behalf as an
indication of guilt. While not alleging any direct comment
by the judge on Joey's failure to testify, Mr. MacPhee alleged that the judge's discussion of the possible defences

available to Joey were, in effect, a comment on Joey's failure to testify at his trial.

His Lordship declined the request. He said that his remarks did not amount to a comment on the failure of the accused to testify and overt comments to the jury could make the situation worse by directly reminding the jury that Joey did not testify on his own behalf.

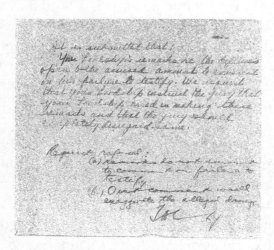

Shortly after midnight Mr. Justice Campbell called the jury in for a report on their progress toward a verdict and they returned to their deliberations. At 1:40 AM, the jury sent the following note to His Lordship:

To His Lordship Chief Justice Thane A. Campbell:

Please instruct the jury as to Court ruling on insanity brought out by drinking alcoholic liquor.

Signed: Elijah Pierce
Foreman of Jury

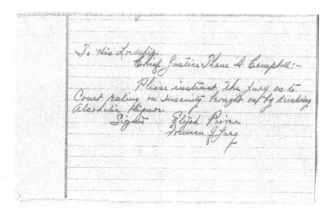

Mr. Justice Campbell provided further instructions on the defence of insanity and the jury resumed their deliberations at 2:25 AM.

At 2:45 AM, the jury returned with the following verdict:

We find that the Accused, who stands charged with having murdered Mary Ann MacKinnon, was insane at the time of the commission of the offence, and we declare that we acquit him of the said offence on account of such insanity.

Signed: Elijah A. Pierce
Foreman of Jury

#7609

THE KING

vs

JOSEPH GABRIEL MacDONALD

We find that the Accused, who stands charged with
having murdered Mary Ann MacKinnon, was insane at the time
of the commission of the offence, and we declare that we
acquit him of the said offence on account of such insanity.

Signed Elijah A Pierce

Foreman of Jury

At the request of the Deputy Attorney General, His Lordship ordered that: "Joseph Gabriel MacDonald be kept in strict custody in the County Jail at Georgetown until the pleasure of the Lieutenant Governor is known".

CHAPTER 7
POST-TRIAL EVENTS

ON AUGUST 21, 1952 the Executive Council of PEI passed an Order-in-Council in the following language:

Pursuant to section 966 of the Criminal Code of Canada, Council did and doth hereby order that Joseph Gabriel McDonald of Chepstow in Kings County, at present confined in Kings County Jail, be committed for safe custody indefinitely to the common jail for Queens County at Charlottetown and that the warrant of His Honour the Lieutenant-Governor do issue accordingly.

His Honour Thomas William Lemuel Prowse signed the following warrant which was co-signed by P.S. Fielding, the Clerk of the Executive Council:

CANADA

PROVINCE OF PRINCE EDWARD ISLAND

Elizabeth the Second by the Grace of God of Great Britain, Ireland and the British Dominions beyond the Seas, Queen, Defender of the Faith. To the Sheriff of Kings County and the Sheriff of Queens County and the Keeper of the common jail for Queens County.

GREETING:

WHEREAS Joseph Gabriel McDonald of Chepstow in Kings County was tried upon indictment for murder at the July 1952 sittings of the Supreme Court at Georgetown upon which trial the verdict of the jury was as follows: "We find that the accused, who stands charged with having murdered Mary Ann MacKinnon, was insane at the time of the commission of the offence, and we declare that we acquit him of the said offence on the account of such insanity".

AND WHEREAS the order of the Court upon such verdict was that the said Joseph Gabriel McDonald be kept in strict custody in the common jail of Kings County until the pleasure of the Lieutenant-Governor is known;

YOU the Sheriffs of Kings and Queens Counties are hereby commanded to take the said Joseph Gabriel McDonald and him safely convey from the common jail for Kings County at Georgetown to the common jail for Queens County at Charlottetown, and you the said keeper of the common jail for Queens County are hereby commanded to keep the said Joseph Gabriel McDonald in safe custody indefinitely in the common jail for Queens County.

CANADA
PROVINCE OF PRINCE EDWARD ISLAND

Elizabeth the Second by the
Grace of God of Great Britain,
Ireland and the British
Dominions beyond the Seas,
Queen, Defender of the Faith.

To the Sheriff of Kings County
and the Sheriff of Queens
County and the Keeper of the
common jail for Queens County.

M.L.A. Bowes
Lieutenant-Governor.

GREETING:

WHEREAS Joseph Gabriel McDonald of Chepstow in Kings County
was tried upon an indictment for murder at the July 1952 sittings of
the Supreme Court at Georgetown upon which trial the verdict of the
jury was as follows: "We find that the accused, who stands charged
with having murdered Mary Ann McKinnon, was insane at the time of the
commission of the offence, and we declare that we acquit him of the
said offence on account of such insanity".

AND WHEREAS the order of the Court upon such verdict was that
the said Joseph Gabriel McDonald be kept in strict custody in the common
jail of Kings County until the pleasure of the Lieutenant-Governor is
known;

YOU the Sheriffs of Kings and Queens Counties are hereby commanded to take the said Joseph Gabriel McDonald and him safely convey from
the common jail for Kings County at Georgetown to the common jail for
Queens County at Charlottetown, and you the said keeper of the common
jail for Queens County are hereby commanded to keep the said Joseph
Gabriel McDonald in safe custody indefinitely in the common jail for
Queens County.

By Command,

P. S. Fielding

Clerk of the Executive Council.

EXECUTIVE COUNCIL _____ August 21, 1952.

UNSATISFIED JUDGMENT FUND
MACDONALDS vs HAYDEN

Further to a Minute of Council dated January 10, 1952 and under the provisions of Part IX of "The Highway Traffic Act", Council did and doth hereby order the payment by the Provincial Treasurer from the Unsatisfied Judgment Fund to Catherine MacDonald and Georgina MacDonald, Judgment Creditors and Lester P. O'Donnell, Solicitor for the Judgment Creditors of the sum of One thousand Dollars ($1,000.00), being the final two-thirds payment of general damages ordered to be paid pursuant to an Order of the Honourable Mr. Justice MacGuigan dated the 12th day of December 1951.

DEPARTMENT OF EDUCATION
ADOPTION OF LAND VALUATIONS IN SCHOOL DISTRICTS OF
MONTGOMERY, SOUTH GRANVILLE, FORTUNE RD., CARTIER AND VICTORIA CROSS

Pursuant to Section 79 (a) of "The Public School Act", Council did and doth hereby order that the valuation of the properties within the undermentioned School Districts, as prepared by the Land Valuation Board and filed with the Department of Education this date, be adopted by the School Trustees of the said School Districts,-

> Montgomery School District
> South Granville School District
> Fortune Road School District
> Cartier School District
> Victoria Cross School District

RE JOSEPH GABRIEL MCDONALD

Pursuant to section 966 of the Criminal Code of Canada, Council did and doth hereby order that Joseph Gabriel McDonald of Chepstow in Kings County, at present confined in Kings County jail, be committed for safe custody indefinitely to the common jail for Queens County at Charlottetown and that the warrant of His Honour the Lieutenant-Governor do issue accordingly.

GRANT - - LITTLE THEATRE GUILD

Council did and doth hereby approve the payment of a grant of Two hundred Dollars ($200.00) to the Little Theatre Guild of Charlottetown for the fiscal year ending March 31st, 1953.

OVERTIME PAYMENT - LOUIS F. McMURRER

Council did and doth hereby approve the payment of the sum of Seventy-two Dollars ($72.00) to Louis F. McMurrer of the Duplicating Branch for overtime work in connection with the printing of Correspondence Courses for the Department of Education.

DEPARTMENT OF PUBLIC WORKS AND HIGHWAYS
ADDITIONAL APPROPRIATION

Council did and doth hereby approve the following additional appropriation for the fiscal year ending March 31st, 1953,-

	Present	Additional	Total
Federal-Provincial Highway Projects	$600,000.	$120,000.	$720,000.

The Supreme Court of PEI, which had been adjourned following the murder trial, resumed its sitting on September 23, 1952 with Chief Justice Campbell presiding and S.S. Hessian, QC acting for the Crown. The first case called was the rape charge against Joseph Gabriel MacDonald and, again H.F. MacPhee, QC represented the accused. The Crown made a motion for a stay of proceedings on the rape charge and the court granted the motion.

These are the last official documents the author could locate with respect to the legal proceedings against Joey. Despite diligent searching of all possible sources of information, staff at the PEI Public Archives and records office have been unable to document when and under what authority Joey was released from the Queens County Jail. Staff searched the records housed at Public Archives and at Government House. The Queens County Jail has been replaced and is now privately owned. Although there was legislation governing the retention of certain records when the jail was closed, the province did not have a formal records management system in place and the records appear to have been destroyed.

Although the duration of Joey's incarceration in the Queens County Jail cannot be established with certainty, some interesting information has survived. My uncle Dickie Power (who was married to Joey's sister Mary Ellen) visited Joey a number of times while he was in Queens County Jail and told people that Joey had a relationship with the head jailer such that he was not being treated like a prisoner.

THE NEW QUEEN'S COUNTY JAIL—CHARLOTTETOWN

P.E.I. Public Archives and Records Office
Photo ID Number: P0006825,   Accession Number: Acc4352/s2/ss1/5788-1

Current photo of the former Queens County Jail.

Other unconfirmed anecdotal information suggests that Joey worked on the head jailer's personal property on weekends and, as I will discuss later, the jailer might have taken Joey with him for a Sunday visit to David MacKinnon's foster family's residence.

A relative of the head jailer told me that his name was Lloyd Simpson and Lloyd was married to Margaret (Marg) whose maiden name was Reid. Marg Simpson's brother and sister lived with the Simpsons at the time that Joey was in custody at the Queens County Jail. The jailer's relative told me that she gave one of her nephews a DNA kit as a Christmas present and he searched his family tree and discovered that the head jailer's sister-in-law (Marg Simpson's sister who had lived with the head jailer) had a daughter in 1954 and that DNA had established that Joey was the father. The jailer's relative was surprised to be contacted by a cousin she had never heard of. This relative was able to establish that Lloyd Simpson had a priest make arrangements for her aunt to go to a Convent in Quebec where she had the baby and gave her up for adoption. The child's mother returned to PEI, married, and had three sons but never told her parents or children about having a child and giving her up for adoption. That part of the story has a happy ending with Joey's daughter eventually becoming acquainted with her half-brothers and other family members she had not known about. It appears that Joey was aware that he had a daughter. The head jailer's relative told me that Joey called the Reid residence one evening and another sister answered the phone and Joey asked to speak to the child's mother. The sister who answered the phone refused to let Joey speak to her sister and told him to never call again. When her parents (who were unaware of Joey's relationship with a family member) asked who had called, the sister stated that it was a 'wrong number'.

It is known that Joey was 'exiled' from PEI and lived in the Lower Mainland of British Columbia until he died on April 17, 2011 at the age of 84. His father, Aeneas MacDonald, died on March 18, 1953 and it is reported that he attended his father's funeral under escort by an unknown agency. Joey's sister, Mabel MacDonald, believes that he was still in the Queens County Jail at the time of his father's death and that his escort was the head of the institution where he was incarcerated. His mother, Catherine 'Katie' MacDonald, died in 1972 and Joey reportedly attended her funeral unescorted.

In an interview on November 27, 1951, Estelle MacKinnon told Cpl. Strong that Thomas J. Kickham, MP [later Senator Thomas J. Kickham], the Member of Parliament for Kings County [since expanded geographically and renamed Cardigan] had written a letter to her mother and visited her personally asking her to agree to have the rape charge reduced. The author's personal knowledge indicates that Joey came from an excellent family and his conduct in these matters was starkly in contrast with that of the rest of his family. It would not be surprising to have the local Member of Parliament lobby for leniency or to intercede on his behalf to have him released from custody. It is likely that Joey's family agreed to him living in British Columbia for the remainder of his life as a condition of his being released from the Queens County Jail.

The author's family believed that Joey had received the royal prerogative of mercy with a condition that he reside in British Columbia and never return to PEI. This is a rarely used remedy which permits Her Majesty to cancel the imprisonment of any person who is serving a sentence under an Act of Parliament. Her Majesty's authority to grant the royal prerogative is unlimited by any other provision of the *Criminal Code*. Without a conviction having been entered on either the rape or the murder charge, it is an interesting legal issue as to whether or not Joey was 'serving a sentence under the authority of an Act of Parliament' which is the prerequisite for the royal prerogative of mercy. Since Joey was not convicted of any offence, the rape charge was stayed (in effect, withdrawn) by the Crown, and he was acquitted of the murder charge by reason of insanity, meaning that he might not have been imprisoned for any violation of a federal statute. As such, the royal prerogative of mercy would not be available to release him from the Queens County Jail unless his detention because of his alleged insanity could be considered as a "sentence under an Act of Parliament". It is unlikely that Joey's lawyer and his political supporter(s) would attempt to advance such a tenuous proposition to secure his release from custody and they would seek his release by some other means. In the absence of the availability of the royal prerogative of mercy, Joey's release must have been accomplished by some other means. The apparent absence of any official documentation of how Joey was released from the Queens County Jail, and the terms and conditions of his exile (if any), is strongly suggestive of there having been a quiet agreement among the persons involved in the matter (which did not include members of the MacKinnon family) to allow for his release from custody with the requirement that Joey had to live in British Columbia and never return to Prince Edward Island.

CHAPTER 8
LIFE IN EXILE

BECAUSE OF THE unavailability of documentation surrounding Joey's release from the Queens County Jail, it is unknown when he was released and under what conditions. But it is likely that he was released in 1954 and he lived the remainder of his life in British Columbia.

While living in BC, Joey maintained contact with PEI residents by telephone. He reportedly made reasonably regular calls to his former neighbour in Chepstow, Joey 'Joey Syl Joe' MacDonald. Unfortunately, 'Joey Syl' MacDonald died before research for this book began. He also called Mary Ann's nephew, Frankie MacAulay, including one thoughtful call when Frankie had returned home from hospitalization following a heart attack. Frankie died in 2016 apparently without learning much about Joey's life in BC. He did mention that Joey had described the perils of driving large trucks hauling loads of logs on single-lane logging roads with sharp turns and over mountainous terrain and remarked that a person would need to be 'half crazy' to do such work.

Joey's older sister, Mabel MacDonald, who was married and living on Souris Line Road at the time of these events, said that Joey called her on special occasions, such as family birthdays, while he lived in BC. Mabel reported that Joey was always interested in what people he knew were doing especially in the farming and fishing industry. He seemed to have a lot of knowledge about current activities on PEI and he had a keen interest in politics and current events. Joey did not divulge much about himself during these conversations and, if asked, he would only provide a general answer with no detail. She remembers him attending their father's funeral in 1953 under escort but she does not remember if he attended their mother's funeral in 1972. Mabel remembers that Joey developed a close relationship with the jailer at the Queens County Jail and his family and that he did some work for the jailer's son at his residence.

Joey also called his niece, Margaret Ching, several times a year. He mentioned to her that he worked in the lumber industry in Squamish, BC but, when Margaret visited him in 1986, he was living in Vancouver. Joey did not reveal much about himself in these calls, providing only general non-informative responses to questions about his activities. As with others he spoke to, he seemed knowledgeable about and interested in PEI activities especially farming and fishing. He usually called early in the morning Pacific Time and indicated that he had been reading the local newspaper.

Joey's nephew, Edward Power, first met him in 1972 when Joey was working as a lumber grader in the Lower Mainland of BC. Edward learned that Joey had worked in the lumber industry in Squamish but had also worked in the lumber industry for a considerable time in the Lower Mainland until he retired at about age 65. Joey was born on November 2, 1927 so that would have been in about 1992. Joey seemed well connected in the lumber industry and he called someone and Edward immediately had a job on the green chain of a mill on northern Vancouver Island.

Edward associated with Joey socially in the Vancouver area with occasional trips to Point Roberts and Bellingham, Washington. He said that Joey never smoked, was a social drinker but later stopped using alcohol completely, and he never married. Joey lived in the Granville area of Vancouver and he died in 2011 at the age of 84.

Edward stated that Joey was an avid newspaper reader, he loved sports and politics, and he described him as very intelligent and "a good man". Edward returned to the Maritimes but maintained contact with Joey until Joey died.

Joey lived in an apartment building in the South Granville area of Vancouver from approximately 1985 until his death in 2011. He was quite reclusive and did not appear to have much social interaction with other residents of the building or outside the building. One long-term building resident told the author that Joey's closest friend in the building had passed away. This resident said that Joey did not spend much time in the building but spent a lot of time in his car parked on shopping centre parking lots apparently listening to the radio. He also stated that Joey had two knee surgeries and that he died of a blood clot several days after the second procedure. Another person told the author that he became acquainted with Joey when the person visited others in the apartment building where Joey lived. He took Joey to the hospital for his second knee surgery and drove him home from the hospital. Joey was anxious to be released from the hospital and return to his residence and he might have been discharged too early causing the blood clot. This acquaintance also described Joey as being reclusive. He stated that he volunteered to be a pall bearer at Joey's funeral in a Catholic church in Vancouver and said that Joey was buried in the Catholic cemetery in Surrey, BC.

Joey was buried in the Gardens of Gethsemani, 15604 32nd Avenue, Surrey, British Columbia and his headstone contains insignia commemorating his membership in Local 1-71 of the International Woodworkers of America and the Roman Catholic fraternal order The Knights of Columbus.

Rt. Rev. Stanley, Galvon, Archdiocese of Vancouver.

Over the years there have been some anecdotal reports of Islanders having chance meetings with Joey and some of his acquaintances in British Columbia. All of these encounters produced very positive reports of Joey's life in exile and included indications that he led a crime-free life and was a charitable man. Joey's life in British Columbia vindicated the unique sentence that the PEI justice system had crafted especially for him.

When one compares the climate, employment opportunities, accessibility to professional sports and other forms of entertainment of PEI to the Lower Mainland of British Columbia, the Lower Mainland wins every category.

Using only such comparisons, it is easy to conclude that 'Joey got away with murder'. But there are other considerations which must be examined in order to reach a valid conclusion on the issue of whether Joey received a reward or was punished. Maritimers are notably clannish and Joey was no exception. Being sent as far away from his home and family as Canadian geography permits with orders to never return, even for a short visit, is punishment. This is especially so for a farm boy from PEI whose expectation growing up was to continue living on the family farm, close to most of his relatives. Arriving in British Columbia, all alone with no support of any kind, must have been quite a devastating experience especially since it was not his choice and there was no option to return.

He appears to have managed the challenges quite well by obtaining accommodation and employment and achieving success in the lumber industry. Although exiled, he appears to have maintained an enduring interest in PEI as evidenced by his efforts to maintain contact with PEI residents and his interest in news and events on PEI. It is perhaps fair to say that Joey actually received a life sentence.

CHAPTER 9
MACKINNON FAMILY AFTER MARY ANN

WHEN MARY ANN DIED, she left eleven orphan children. Her husband, John Charles (J.C.) MacKinnon had died of a heart attack on the same date she died, two years earlier.

Family members decided where the children would go. Mary Ann's brother, Albert, who was a bachelor farmer living about four miles away on Souris Line Road, took in the five oldest; Estelle, Alban (Obie), Aelred (Mac), Alice, and Danny, as well as seven-year-old Betty who was his godchild. The other five children; Margie, Maureen, Justin, Kenny, and David went to other families who offered to help but none was formally adopted. Mary Ann had another son, James Augustus, who was born on May 30, 1933 but died on May 20, 1934.

The MacKinnon house was vacant until the spring of 1953 when Obie moved into the now empty 'Old House' as it is affectionately known. With considerable energy and assistance from his neighbours, he revived the homestead. The house had been built on the 1800s and had been a stop for Bishop Bernard Angus MacEachern during his missionary work. The legendary bishop said Mass at the house several times. Margie moved the house closer to the shore where it is still used as a seasonal home and Obie built a house on its original site. The 200-acre property is scenically situated on MacKinnon Point and it is the location of Justin's home. As well, seven of his siblings and some of Mary Ann's grandchildren have homes or cottages on the property.

Mary Estelle, who readers are now quite familiar with, was born on May 7, 1932. When her mother died, Estelle abandoned her registered nursing program and resumed teaching – first on Souris Line Road. Then she moved back to the "Old House" and taught at Little Harbour School. She married a successful farmer, Bernard MacAulay, who raised purebred Yorkshire pigs and engaged in mixed farming on the farm adjacent to her Uncle Albert's farm. Bernard's parents, Frank and Marguerite

MacAulay, were not related to Mary Ann but they had informally adopted Albert as a child, raised him, and got him established on the adjacent farm. Estelle and Bernard raised a family of eight, Anne, Allan, Gerard, Brian, Edward, Ian, Bernardine, and Terry. After raising her family, Estelle worked as a nursing assistant in the Colville Manor (a senior's residence) in Souris retiring in 1997. She currently resides near some of her grandchildren in Charlottetown.

Alban Joseph (Obie) was born on August 28, 1934 and died as a result of a farm tractor accident on September 22, 2008. Obie only spent a few months with Uncle Albert then he moved back to Little Harbour and lived briefly with Jimmy MacPhee and He worked with Jimmy's brother, Sept, cutting and storing ice (for use on offshore fishing draggers to refrigerate catches between the fishing grounds and the processing plant). He moved back into the 'Old House' and started a mixed farming operation that included growing potatoes, grain, and hay and raising some dairy cattle. He also fished lobsters in season until 2000, had a trucking business and operated a custom spraying business spraying crops for neighbouring farmers. Obie married Margie Clinton of Souris Line Road in 1971 and they had three children; Ronnie, Sharon, and Darren.

Margie, who formerly worked for Usen Fisheries Ltd. in Souris until a fire destroyed the plant in 1993, lives in the family home in Little Harbour.

John Aelred (Mac) was born on October 18, 1935 and died on March 24, 2011. Mac had been living with Uncle Albert before his mother's death and was attending St. Dunstan's University in Charlottetown. After university, Mac obtained employment with Canada Packers in Toronto. He married a teacher, Rosemary Price, of Priceville, New Brunswick and they moved to Calgary and Brooks, Alberta where he continued working in the meat-packing industry overseeing the construction of and managing a large plant in Brooks. They moved back to Calgary where Mac was a realtor for several years. Mac and Rosemary had four sons; Robert, John, Danny, and Michael. Rosemary died on October 24, 2012.

Alice Pauline was born on November 17, 1936 and died on September 29, 1988. Alice lived with Uncle Albert briefly then moved to Halifax, Nova Scotia and worked as a 'nanny'. In 1953 she moved back to the homestead and worked with Obie getting the farming business started. She and Obie are considered to be the 'rocks of the family' for the love and guidance they provided to their siblings. Alice married Roland Bushey of Souris Line Road. They lived in the homestead until they built a new house in Chepstow in 1966. Roland is a heavy equipment operator who was originally employed by Curran & Briggs of Summerside and is now, at the age of 90, employed by Chapman Brothers Construction of Souris. Alice and Roland had four children; Charlene, Kent, Lisa, and Jeff.

Danny Stanclause was born on January 10, 1938. Danny lived with Uncle Albert until 1953 when he moved back to the homestead. He joined the Canadian Army in 1957 in London, Ontario and served three years and acquired the trade of welder. He worked as a pipeline welder in a number of places around the world, then returned to London and started his own welding business, Curney Construction, working mainly on pipelines and other construction projects. He married Carole MacLean of London and they had two children; Shari and Shawn. Danny died on July 19, 2020.

Margaret Beatrice (Margie) was born on November 13, 1939 and died of cancer on November 18, 1995. After her mother died, Margie spent three years with her aunt and uncle Mildred and Frank MacAulay in Halifax, Nova Scotia. She then returned to the homestead and completed high school at St. Mary's Convent then a two-year nursing course at Hillsborough Hospital in Charlottetown. Following graduation in 1960, she moved to Calgary, lived with her brother Mac, and worked at Grace Hospital. She married Wilf Obethier and they moved to Regina, Saskatchewan where Wilf worked in human resources at the Grey Nuns Hospital. In 1970, the family moved to Ottawa, Ontario where Wilf worked for the Government of Canada. Margie returned to nursing and worked at the Children's Hospital of Eastern Ontario. The had four children: Mary Ann, John, Peggy, and Karen. Wilf is retired and lives in Ottawa.

Anna Maureen was born on December 2, 1940. After her mother's death, Maureen and Justin lived with Wilfred and Mary Ann MacDonald of St. Andrew's, PEI.

The MacDonalds operated a small mixed farm and Wilfred also worked for the Canadian National Railroad. In 1958, Maureen returned to the homestead and finished her education at Souris Regional High School. She worked at the telephone office in Souris until 1963. Maureen married Francis Howlett of Gowan Brae, PEI in 1961. They lived with the Howlett family until 1966 when they bought a house in Souris West. Francis was a farmer, trucker, lobster fisherman, and, for a period of time, a fur rancher. They had four children: Bernadette, Darlene, Paul, and Shawn. Shawn died in a motor vehicle collision on September 8, 2012 at the age of 37. After raising her children, Maureen completed a Resident Care Worker course at Holland College, Charlottetown and worked at Colville Manor and Eastern Kings Health until retiring in 2006. Francis passed away on February 8, 2020.

Justin Charles was born on August 20, 1943. Justin only lived with the MacDonalds for about four months and was anxious and lonely so Estelle took him to live at Uncle Albert's. He moved back to the homestead in 1953 and worked on the farm and the lobster boat. He worked as a labourer in Ontario for a few years then moved back to Little Harbour. He captained his own lobster boat from 1958 to 2010. Justin married Mae MacPhee of Red Point, PEI and they had four children: Janice, Jansen, Jamie, and Julie. Justin and Mae built a house on the MacKinnon property where they still live. Mae worked as a nurse at Colville Manor and Souris Detox and Mental Community Health until retirement.

Elizabeth Jane (Betty) was born on July 20, 1944 and died on October 8, 2017. Betty lived with Uncle Albert until 1953 when she returned to the homestead. After high school, Betty completed a Licensed Nursing Assistant course at the PEI School of Nursing in 1963. She worked as a Licensed Nursing Assistant for her entire career at the Souris Hospital and Souris Detox. Betty married Gene Fay, a farmer and trucker of East Baltic, PEI. They had three children; Carl, Kevin, and Angela. Gene is retired and lives in East Baltic.

Kenneth Francis (Kenny) was born on June 1, 1946. After his mother died, Kenny went to live with his uncle Charlie and aunt Helen MacAulay in Mount Stewart, PEI. The next year, the family moved briefly to Burnaby, British Columbia, then to Prince George, BC. After high school, Kenny became a heavy equipment mechanic and returned to the homestead and worked for Chapman Brothers Construction. He moved to Newfoundland and met and married Marie Burton of Corner Brook, NL. They had two daughters; Cora Lee and Tana, and subsequently divorced. Kenny moved to Toronto, Ontario and started his own company, Tancor Construction, and spent most of his career doing pipeline work. Kenny is now retired and lives in Brampton, Ontario.

David Lawrence was born on September 4, 1947 and died on February 14, 2016. After his mother died, David went to live with John and Loretta MacMillan of Canavoy, PEI. John was a farmer and Loretta was a part-time worker as a cook at a lobster factory and a cashier in a local grocery store. David lived with the MacMillans until he reached high school age when he moved to Souris to attend Souris Regional High School where he played football and basketball. The MacMillans were friends of the jailer at the Queens County Jail and David told the author that he believes he had supper with Joey one Sunday evening. David remembers the jailer and his wife visiting the MacMillans one Sunday afternoon with an unidentified man with them. David said "there was some adult whispering" the content of which he was not supposed to hear. The guests spent the afternoon and evening with the MacMillans and David believed the unidentified man was Joey. When he was 25, David married Dorothy (Dot) Poole and became a step-father to Dorothy's 14-year old daughter Gail. David and Dot had two children, Craig and Nicole. After 25 years of marriage, Dot died of pancreatic cancer. David became a step-father again when he married Susan Sherwood who had three grown children; Devon, Jessie, and Sarah. I have summarized some of the highlights of David's working life under the heading "Acknowledgements" and I will not repeat the details here.

SOME THOUGHTS

THE OUTCOME OF THE proceedings against Joey were quite 'PEIish'. PEI is more rural and parochial than many parts of Canada and is blessed with a somewhat uncommon civility. In the mid-20th century it was especially so, with the lack of electricity, telephones, and automobiles making neighbours more dependent upon each other. As well, as readers will have noted in the previous chapters, many of the people involved in the criminal proceedings were friends, neighbours, and, in some instances, relatives. This closeness made it difficult for the participants in the criminal proceedings. The jurors were all from Kings County as the law required and, although they were not close associates of any of the parties, they were not far removed geographically. They would have an understandable reluctance to deliver a 'guilty' verdict when the sentence was to "be hanged by the neck until dead". That verdict was subject only to the whims of the federal cabinet which sometimes commuted such sentences to life imprisonment.

With no one advocating for any form of vengeance, and forgiveness being the order of the day, the Crown's suggestion of acquittal by reason of insanity (although the defence was not founded upon any medical evidence of insanity and the accused's physical acts defied any suggestion of alcohol impairment) provided the jury with a route to an outcome they and the community they represented would be comfortable with. It appears that the provincial cabinet likely completed the task by fashioning a remedy, a lifetime expulsion to British Columbia, which met the community's needs of being certain that Joey would never to be in a position to create any future anxiety to Estelle or other members of the MacKinnon family. A truly 'Made in PEI' remedy!

With no documentation discovered that supported Joey's release from the Queens County Jail and his exile to British Columbia, it is a fair assumption that he agreed to the arrangement in order to obtain his liberty. It is an interesting question if Joey would have been free to return to PEI after April 17, 1982. On that date, Canada repatriated its constitution which included an entrenched bill of rights. Being a constitutional document, the *Canadian Charter of Rights and Freedoms* is the supreme law of the country. Parliament is no longer supreme, subsection 52(1) of the Charter provides the courts with the ability to declare any law that is inconsistent with the *Charter* to be "of no force or effect". The *Charter* applies to the government of each province and, presumably, the Government of PEI was a party to the arrangement that required Joey to live in British Columbia. Among the rights in the *Charter* are mobility rights. Paragraph 6(2)(a) of the *Charter* provides a right for every Canadian citizen and permanent resident "to move to and take up residence in any province". As Joey having died in 2011, it is totally moot at this time, but the author sometimes contemplated the possible outcomes should he have asserted his mobility rights following the enactment of the Charter. There are no court decisions with similar factual settings, but the Supreme Court of Canada in *Black v. Law Society of Alberta*, [1989] 1 S.C.R. 591, 58 D.L.R. (4th) 317 stated Section 6 of the Charter must be interpreted generously to achieve its purpose: to protect the rights of citizens and permanent residents to move about the country, to reside where they wish, and to pursue their livelihoods without regard to provincial boundaries. It would have been interesting to see whether or not the arrangement which expelled Joey from PEI would have withstood a constitutional challenge.

This story gives rise to many interesting social questions as well. The story is set at a time and place which can be characterized as a peaceful rural setting in a largely male-dominated society. At the time, lands were almost exclusively registered in the names of men. It wasn't until the Supreme Court of Canada's decisions in *Murdoch v. Murdoch*, [1975] 1 SCR 423 and *Rathwell v. Rathwell*, [1978] 2 SCR 436 that farm wives' contributions to their former husbands' business successes were deemed worthy of compensation on the breakdown of marital relationships. Prior to 1893, PEI had a bicameral legislature consisting of an upper house called the Legislative Council of Prince Edward Island and a lower house called the House of Assembly. The two houses were merged in 1893 and the assembly was then made up of fifteen dual constituencies (five in each of the three counties) – each with a "Councillor" and an "Assemblyman". Only land owners could vote for a Councillor prior to 1963. At the time of these events, all members of grand and petit juries were required to be male and all members of the legal profession and the judiciary were men. As well, most of the criminal prosecutions were against men and there was only one federal prison for women in Canada.

In addition to being deprived of property rights, some voting rights, the right to serve on juries, and their almost complete absence from the legal profession, women of the mid-20th century were expected to be submissive in many respects and play the often unrecognized role of supporting their husbands and raising the children. (Ironically, the courts used the important role of raising children as the rationale for excluding women from jury duty.) Mary Ann and Estelle found themselves in that type of society where women's voices were generally not heard. The crime of rape was not something that either had any real knowledge of and their first instinct was to seek advice from their pastor who correctly directed them to the police who then proceeded with the appropriate investigation including a somewhat delayed medical examination. Unlike many other women of her generation, Mary Ann became an assertive advocate for justice. She assisted the police in their investigation and vigorously resisted the political efforts to dispose of the rape charge in some 'out of court' manner. Joey was a product of this male-dominated environment and probably expected that the matter could be settled without any formal court proceedings or jeopardy to his liberty. As well, he was raised in a household that had relatives in Boston, Massachusetts who sent newspapers from Boston to their former home which Joey read and which likely made him more aware of but less sensitive to significant criminal activity. These circumstances make it quite admirable that a Convent-educated woman would pursue the rape charge with such vigour that it became the motive for her murder.

It is perhaps time to ponder how much our society has advanced, if any, since the events chronicled here. Women in PEI now have equal voting and property rights, serve on juries, and are represented in the legal profession and the judiciary but have they achieved full equality?

ACKNOWLEDGEMENTS

MARY ANN'S YOUNGEST SON, David MacKinnon had planned to document some of the details of his mother's life and death in a book but, unfortunately, he died in Burnaby, BC on February 14, 2016 at the age of 68. David had a varied and adventurous life in which he worked on a fishing vessels out of Souris, PEI, Riverport, Petit-de-Grat, and Lunenburg, Nova Scotia, was an organizer for the United Fishermen and Allied Workers Union in Nova Scotia and the Newfoundland Fisherman's Union as well as working on union organizing campaigns as varied as Michelin Tire in Nova Scotia and Syncrude in Alberta. He also was a staff representative for the British Columbia Service Employees Union and an industrial relations officer with the British Columbia Ministry of Labour. He was active politically as the co-manager of a campaign that saw the first NDP Member of Parliament elected in Newfoundland and served as treasurer and president of the federal New Democratic Party. He also ran as a candidate for the NDP in the federal constituency of Cardigan [PEI]. David was the ultimate champion of the underdog. During particularly difficult negotiations to achieve a first collective agreement for fish plant workers in Newfoundland where the employer was more interested in defeating the union than bargaining in good faith, his relatives sent him money for food because he was giving what he had to the striking workers who he considered worse off than himself. Although he did not get started writing the book he intended to write, David collected a number of documents which his sister, Maureen Howlett, provided to this author which were most helpful in writing this book.

These documents included some of Mary Ann's writings including some of her submissions to the Charlottetown Patriot under the Mrs. Wiggs pseudonym and accounts of the preliminary hearing and murder trial published contemporaneously in the Charlottetown Patriot. In addition to providing the documents that David had assembled, Maureen provided the author with summaries of her own life and the lives of her siblings which are recorded in Chapter 9.

My niece, Patricia MacAulay, BA, BEd, RCAT, MA provided me with some thoughtful sociological insight into Mary Ann's unusual strength of character which I hope I have adequately conveyed to our readers. Mary Ann was a feminist when feminism was virtually unknown on PEI.

The author is also indebted to Hon. George Mullally, QC a retired judge of the Supreme Court of Prince Edward Island. Hon. Mr. Mullally articled with the law firm which represented Joey during the legal proceedings related to the rape and murder charges. One of his early duties with the firm was the destruction of inactive records including the firm's files on the rape and murder proceedings. Thankfully, he preserved the transcript of the preliminary hearing from the rape charge which provided the author with authoritative details of this proceeding.

Pursuant to a request under the *Access to Information* Act, Library and Archives Canada provided the author with a CD containing RCMP file 51-HQ-681-L-1 which they received from the RCMP on June 1, 2015.

This material provided the author with an accurate and contemporaneous account of the RCMP's involvement in the investigation of the murder and the subsequent criminal proceedings.

The author also received splendid cooperation from staff at the Public Archives and Records Office of Prince Edward Island who provided access to and copies of documents relating to the preliminary hearing and trial of the murder charge. The file contains a 3-volume transcript of the preliminary hearing, the official documents relating to the indictment, and such things as the prosecutor's handwritten notes taken during the trial. While PEI Public Archives staff were able to locate the Order-in-Council authorizing the transfer from the Kings County Jail to the Queens County Jail and the associated Lieutenant Governor's warrant, their diligent efforts did not locate any documentation that revealed the authority for and the terms of Joey's release from the Queens County Jail.

Astute readers will note an apparent inconsistency in the spelling of Mary Ann's middle name. The PEI Public Archives have typewritten index cards of names and dates of birth that were prepared from hand-written baptismal records. Mary Ann MacAulay's card shows that she was born on November 4, 1909 and Rev. Donald B. MacDonald baptized her on November 7, 1909. It appears that Mary Ann preferred to add an 'e' to her middle name (likely because of her affection for the red-headed orphan in Lucy Maude Montgomery's classic novel *Anne of Green Gables*) and a few of the legal documents have spelled her middle name with an 'e'. Throughout the book, the author used the legal spelling of her middle name but, where it was spelled 'Anne' in her writings or in documents that were quoted, the author used the exact spelling that occurred in the original document.

The Robertson Library of the University of Prince Edward Island has digitized copies of most issues of the *Guardian* from December 17, 1890 to December 31, 1964 on a searchable database which is accessible at: **www.island-newspapers.ca/home.** *Guardian* reporters covered the preliminary hearing and trial of the murder charge which provided the author with contemporaneously recorded information on these events. The daily reporting of the legal proceedings was consistent between the Guardian and the Patriot articles that the author had access to. Overall, the information form the various sources was consistent leaving the author with confidence in the veracity of the information provided in this book.

The author also wishes to acknowledge and thank Ann Thurlow of Acorn Press for her major contribution to this book. Ann very patiently, knowledgeably and skillfully transformed what was an overly technical manuscript that would have been comprehensible only to the police and legal community to a more enriched and universally comprehensible story.

ABOUT THE AUTHOR

Ernie MacAulay was born and raised in St. Catherine's, PEI and is the nephew of the case's victim, Mary Ann MacKinnon. He has a Bachelor's of Business Administration from Wilfrid Laurier University, a Bachelor of Law degree and a Master's in Business Administration from the University of Windsor, and worked in federal policing and commercial crime investigations units for much of his career. As a member of the RCMP, he filled a variety of roles including Officer in Charge of the Vancouver Commercial Crime Section and Officer in Charge of Richmond Detachment.

This law enforcement background, combined with dedicated academic research and ancestral history, has formed the basis for Ernie's insights into the legal issues at the heart of this story. He retired from the RCMP in 2001 and currently lives in Charlottetown with his wife Ruth.